THE ILLUSTRATED FRANKENSTEIN

THE ILLUSTRATED
FRANKENSTEIN
JOHN STOKER

Sterling Publishing Co., Inc. New York

Published in 1980 by
Sterling Publishing Co., Inc.
Two Park Avenue
New York, N.Y. 10016

The author and publishers would like to thank the National Film Archive/Stills Library, London, for the stills reproduced on pages 21, 24, 30, 31, 37, 38, 40, 41, 43, 44, 45 (below), 46, 47, 48, 52 (above), 53, 54, 55, 59 (above), 66 (below), 69 (above), 72, 78, 82 (above), 85, 86, 87 (above), 92, 94, 98, 103, 105, 106, 107, 114 and 115.

Published in association with David & Charles UK
First published in Australia and New Zealand 1980
A. H. & A. W. REED PTY LTD
53 Myoora Road, Terrey Hills, Sydney
65-67 Taranaki Street, Wellington 3
also at
Auckland and Christchurch

© John Stoker 1980

National Library of Australia
Cataloguing-in-publication data:
Stoker, John
The illustrated Frankenstein.

Index
ISBN 0 589 50171 2
1. Frankenstein Films — History and Criticism.
2. Frankenstein in Literature.
3. English Fiction — 19th Century — History and Criticism.
4. English Fiction — 20th Century — History and Criticism.
I. Title.
791.43'09'09351

Printed in the United States of America

For my grandmother, Jane Holst, who introduced me to
the world of fantasy films; for my wife, Olwen, who has
been forced to share innumerable horror films with me and
has never flinched once; and for my daughter, Jennie,
whose sympathy for the Monster would have gladdened
the heart of Boris Karloff

Contents

Introduction 9

1 The Birth of the Monster 11

2 The Monster Treads the Boards 15

3 The Silent Monster and his Friends 19

4 The Universal Years 27

5 A Feast of British Blood 49

6 Teenage Monsters Unite 65

7 More British and even some Continental Blood 83

8 Down Mexico Way and Further 95

9 The Television Age 101

10 Short Stories and Novels 113

Conclusion 119

Filmography 120

Bibliography 123

Acknowledgements 123

Index 124

FAMOUS

MONSTERS

OF FILMLAND

A WARREN MAGAZINE

2/6

"FRANKENSTEIN CONQUERS THE WORLD"

Introduction

This book represents an attempt to explore the Frankenstein myth from Mary Shelley to the present day. It is a story that begins on a stormy night in 1816 and appears to have no ending, for the tale of *Frankenstein* is as indestructible as the Monster itself.

My own fascination with the Frankenstein story began when I was nine. At that time I was taken on Saturday night trips to a local cinema in Sunderland called the Roker. On one of those excursions we were told that the film playing on the following evening was for adults only. Immediately a ripple of excitement ran through the audience as the title *The Bride of Frankenstein* flashed on the screen. I was seven years too young for that screening and the following night I envied those who were able to attend the performance. What horrors had they witnessed? What unspeakable deeds had been enacted on the screen? Just what was it all about?

My grandmother, who was a great cinema fan, told me that many years before she had seen a film called *Frankenstein* in which a scientist had created a Monster with disastrous results. It was one of the most terrifying films she had ever seen and was not fit entertainment for a nine-year-old. This film fascinated me and I endeavoured to find out more about it.

I learned that the film was based on a book, and a rather prim librarian was shocked when I placed an order for it. A few days later I collected the book and, with great excitement, began to read it, but after about 30 pages I gave up. Surely this was not the stuff that nightmares were made of. The book was returned to the library and my fascination with Frankenstein ebbed. But I was still interested in fantasy and read such authors as H. G. Wells, Algernon Blackwood, and even Bram Stoker.

By the time I was 13 I was attempting with friends to gain admittance to "X"-certificate horror films. At first I was unsuccessful, but one summer evening I managed to get into the Palladium Cinema in Durham and saw *Return of the Fly*. The floodgates were open and a few weeks later I watched *Frankenstein's Daughter*. It was, on reflection, a dreadful film, but it did rekindle my interest in the myth.

My appetite had been whetted by an American magazine called *Famous Monsters of Filmland*, which ran articles on classic horror films. When I was 16 the Rank Organization saw fit to revive the 1931 version of *Frankenstein* and I made a special Saturday afternoon trip to the Stoll Cinema in Newcastle. I was astonished by what I saw. Here was a film whose power to terrify had not lessened over the years. But the greatest revelation was the performance of Boris Karloff, who created a creature to be pitied. That was the spark that made me tackle the book for the second time, and I now began to appreciate Mary Shelley's novel.

When I went to college in Kent I was once again fortunate, for the National Film Theatre began to revive many of the old Universal horror films. Then there was the Classic Cinema circuit, whose pro-grammers appeared to have a liking for Boris Karloff and double-billed many of his finest films. The Classic in Kilburn yielded *House of Frankenstein* and *Son of Dracula*, while the Classic in Croydon offered, at long last, *The Bride of Frankenstein*. I travelled to Brighton to catch a Classic double-bill of *Frankenstein* and the Bela Lugosi version of *Dracula*. Then, one memorable afternoon, I visited the Granada in Tooting for the revival of *Son of Frankenstein* and *Frankenstein meets the Wolfman*.

Since then I have managed to track down most classics of the fantasy cinema. Although I have spent many exciting hours in this pursuit, I have also had to wade through a vast amount of rubbish, for, sad to say, the glorious names of Frankenstein and Dracula have found themselves attached to some dire productions.

If Mary Shelley were alive today she would be astonished to see how her creation has progressed. She saw her book transferred to the stage and the novel go from success to success, but she could never have dreamt that children would be building copies of her creature from plastic kits.

The strength of the Frankenstein myth is evident from the number of writers, film and television producers, and publishers who have found renewed inspiration from this most compelling of stories. In the following pages you can judge for yourself just how successful they have been.

So, wait no longer. A cloud masks the sky, the thunder rolls, and in a distant castle turret a weird flashing light can be seen. Nature howls her defiance as a young man prepares to flaunt her secrets. Beneath a sheet on an operating table a hand stirs. Who knows what secrets the night still holds?

Famous Monsters of Filmland, the most successful monster magazine of all time *(Warren Publishing)*

1 The Birth of the Monster

When Mary Shelley came to write *Frankenstein* in the summer of 1816 it was not, as many people supposed, merely the product of a competition to write a ghost story. Until that time Mary's life had been a series of uncertainties and setbacks that, sooner or later, were to fuse with her hopes and her fears into the cohesive entity that was *Frankenstein*.

Her mother, Mary Wollstonecraft, had died shortly after giving birth to Mary, leaving her father, William Godwin, to bring up two children. Later Godwin entered into a second marriage, but his new wife not only provided him with a larger family, but also took a hand in his financial affairs and brought him to the brink of ruin.

Mary's only release from the gloomy household occurred when she was sent to Scotland to stay with a family that had befriended her father. On her return to London in the summer of 1814 Mary fell under the spell of the young poet, Percy Bysshe Shelley, who was attempting to help her father out of his financial problems. Shelley greatly admired Godwin, who was a leading radical philosopher and author, and also became attracted to Mary. The two lovers would meet at Mary Wollstonecraft's grave, and later the poet, who was already married, eloped with Mary and her half-sister, Claire. They fled to the continent, but when their money ran out they returned to England where they were shunned by Mary's parents. Tragedy came when the couple's first child died, but later when Shelley's finances began to improve, the poet took his wife to Torquay where she recovered her health.

Meanwhile, Claire, who was attempting to embark on a theatrical career, had met and fallen in love with Lord Byron, and when the notorious nobleman eventually decided to leave the country and settle in Geneva she returned to Mary and Shelley and suggested that they should all visit Switzerland. Shelley had longed to meet Byron and Mary was eager to see Switzerland again, so the couple, together with their new baby William, joined Claire in a second journey to the continent.

The journey to Switzerland was long and laborious. The weather was particularly bad for the time of year and the travellers were much relieved when they eventually reached Geneva. Once again Switzerland gave them all a feeling of elation that could not have been achieved elsewhere. They moved into Dejean's Hôtel d'Angleterre at Secheron, and a few days later they discovered that Lord Byron had arrived.

The poets' first meeting was an uplifting experience for both of them. They not only discovered that they had much in common, but developed a mutual respect for each other that flowered into admiration. The bond of friendship that they struck up lasted until Shelley's death.

The Shelleys soon moved to the Villa Chapuis to avoid the tourists and sightseers who clamoured to see the renowned poets. Byron was a constant visitor to the house and he was always attended by his personal physician, Dr John Polidori. Polidori was only 20 when he was engaged by Byron. His secret ambition was to be a writer—an ambition that had received something of a boost when a publisher had offered him £500 if he could write a book about his employer. He was a handsome young man, but intensely jealous of Byron and Shelley, failing to understand why neither poet treated him as an equal. Byron, whose sense of humour could be cruel on occasions, regarded Polidori's literary ambitions with contempt and constantly taunted him about his writing. But Polidori's part in the creation of Frankenstein was to be an important one.

Not long after Shelley had moved house, Byron decided that he too must find new accommodation and he rented the Villa Diodati, which was next to the Villa Chapuis. In the days that followed a bond developed between Byron, Shelley, and Mary. Evening conversations sparkled with wit and intelligence, and Polidori was frustrated in not being able to play a major part in them.

But one night Polidori managed to introduce the topic of the supernatural into the conversation, a subject that fascinated nineteenth-century man. The secrets of nature were just beginning to be grasped, the strange force of electricity was a phenomenon that had yet to be successfully harnessed, and experiments in galvanism were all the rage.

The weather had taken another turn for the worse and the atmosphere was exactly right for stories of ghostly deeds. The supernatural captured the imagination of the assembled company in the Villa Diodati, and a copy of *Fantasmagoriana* was produced. This popular German work was a collection of horrific stories, and Byron and Shelley found it vastly entertaining. Later in the evening, Byron read from Coleridge's *Christabel* with the most alarming results. Polidori described the consequences in his diary:

> Twelve o'clock really began to talk ghostly. LB repeated some verses of Coleridge's *Christabel*, of the witch's breast; when silence ensued, and Shelley suddenly shrieking and putting his hands to his head, ran out of the room with a candle.

Shelley's outburst had been occasioned by Coleridge's

description of the witch Geraldine, who wishes to possess the young girl, Christabel, and undresses in front of her. While listening to the poem, Shelley had been gazing at his wife and become the victim of a vivid hallucination. Polidori's diary continues:

> Threw water in his face, and after gave him ether. He was looking at Mrs S, and suddenly thought of a woman he had heard of who had eyes instead of nipples, which taking hold of his mind, horrified him.

Shelley's outburst startled the company but it also kindled an idea: surely that atmosphere must inspire some work of literature. They decided that each of them should write a ghost story that would stand comparison with the tales they had read that night. Byron decided to tackle a story of vampirism, while Shelley attempted to draw on his childhood for inspiration. Polidori's tale featured a female monster, although he found difficulty in developing the plot. But Mary was completely devoid of inspiration and failed to write anything.

Byron and Shelley pursued the subject of the supernatural. They were also interested in new scientific developments and one night their conversation turned to the secret of life itself. Shelley was fascinated by the work of Erasmus Darwin, and had himself investigated the force of electricity when he was at Oxford. Mary later wrote:

> Many and long were the conversations between Lord Byron and Shelley to which I was a devout but nearly silent listener. During one of these, various philosophical doctrines were discussed, and among others the nature and principal of life, and whether there was any probability of it ever being discovered or communicated. . . . Perhaps a corpse would be re-animated; galvanism had given token of such things: perhaps the component parts of a creature might be manufactured, brought together, and imbued with vital warmth.

At last Mary was gaining the inspiration to write what would be her most famous story and the most successful tale of those that were born out of that strange summer in Switzerland. The seed had been planted and sleep would nourish and bring forth the reality of *Frankenstein*.

> I saw with shut eyes, but acute mental vision—I saw the pale student of unhallowed arts kneeling beside the thing he had put together—I saw the hideous phantasm of a man stretched out, and then, on the working of some powerful engine, show signs of life, and stir with an uneasy, half vital motion. . . . I wished to exchange the ghastly image of my fancy for the realities around. . . .
> Swift as light and as cheering was the idea that broke in upon me. "I have found it! What terrified me will terrify others; and I need only describe the spectre which had haunted my midnight pillow." On the morrow I announced that I had thought of a story.

At first Mary intended to write only a short story, but Shelley persuaded her that her idea could be expanded into a novel. Her story was set in the epic mould and was fashioned on a wide canvas; the influences on the work were many, but the resulting manuscript presented a unique story that was more than just a tale of terror.

The story begins in the lonely wastes of the Arctic. Captain Robert Walton is exploring this barren region when his vessel comes upon the body of a man who is quickly taken aboard. Walton discovers that the man he has plucked from an icy death is Victor Frankenstein, a student of science who appears to have been pursuing some form of creature across the frozen landscape. Later Frankenstein describes to his rescuer the tragic story of his life.

Victor Frankenstein had been an ardent student of medicine and science. He was fascinated by the forces of nature such as lightning, and when he came to study at the University of Ingoldstadt he began to investigate the secrets of life itself. But his greatest ambition was to endow life into a being that he had created from corpses. In this endeavour he had been successful, but the creature he had brought to life had been a revolting monstrosity.

Frankenstein fled from the awesome sight, abdicating all responsibility for his birth and allowing him to find his own way in the world. From then on tragedy dogged Frankenstein's life. Although the student of science preferred to forget the creature to which he had bestowed life, hoping that the Monster might never be seen again, the creature refused to forget his creator.

Much time elapsed before Victor began to suspect that his creature might still be alive. His brother was killed by an unknown hand and although a servant girl was executed after being found guilty of the crime, Victor feared that the murderer had been his own creation and, while roaming through the hills of Switzerland, Frankenstein came face to face with the Monster and realized the truth.

Having been rejected by the world, the creature had rejected mankind. He had learned to speak and had educated himself to a remarkable degree. All that he now desired was love, and he demanded that Frankenstein create a bride for him. In return, the Monster claimed, he would harm no one else. Victor was forced to agree and journeyed to the Orkney Islands to set up a laboratory to construct the new creature. But when he had assembled the new body Victor realized that he might be giving life to a family of monsters and he destroyed the body before animating it. Seeing the destruction, the Monster warned Frankenstein that his vengeance would be terrible: "I will be with you on your wedding night."

The campaign of revenge began with the murder of Frankenstein's friend, Henry Clerval, and for a time Victor was imprisoned on suspicion of being the murderer. Frankenstein's wedding day arrived and during that night, the Monster murdered Victor's bride, Elizabeth. The hunter then became the hunted, and Frankenstein set off to put an end to the creature. The chase had continued nearly halfway around the world when Captain Walton discovered Victor on the ice flow.

Frankenstein finishes his story but, weakened by

Mary Shelley's parents: (*left*) William Godwin in 1802,
from a portrait by James Northcote; (*right*) Mary Godwin
(née Wollstonecraft) from a portrait by John Opie
(*National Portrait Gallery, London*)

Mary Wollstonecraft Shelley in 1841, 25 years after writing
Frankenstein, from a portrait by Rothwell (*National
Portrait Gallery, London*)

his Arctic trek, he dies. A tall figure appears on board the vessel and at last Walton sees Frankenstein's creation. The Monster discovers that he is now truly alone—even the man who gave him life is dead—and in a fit of remorse he announces his intention of destroying himself:

> I shall ascend my funeral pyre triumphantly, and exult in the agony of the torturing flames. The light of that conflagration will fade away; my ashes will be swept into the sea by the winds. My spirit will sleep in peace; or, if it thinks, it will not surely think thus. Farewell.

The Monster climbs through the cabin window and returns to the Arctic wilderness, never to be seen again.

Victor Frankenstein's character bears many resemblances to Shelley's: both men fled from situations they wished to forget, both were impetuous and zealous, and both were passionately interested in science. Mary Shelley placed many of her own fears into the character of the Monster. As a child she had feared loneliness and longed desperately for a loving friendship. The Monster wishes only to exist in society, but society is revolted by his appearance and he is forced to become an antagonist. Mary had never wished to part from her father, but had been compelled to do so for her relationship with Shelley to survive. Mary and her creation were both forced to wander through Europe in search of some hope for the future.

Perhaps the least successful element in the book is the self-education of the Monster. The majority of this education seems to have been gleaned by eaves-dropping, and he certainly seems to have made astonishingly fast progress. The family on which he spies is conveniently provided with a young Arabian girl who must be taught English and when the Monster finally confronts his creator on a Swiss hill-side, his verbal eloquence would do justice to an after-dinner speaker.

Frankenstein was finally published in 1818 by Lackington, Hughes and Company. Shelley had been instrumental in arranging the publication and even wrote the introduction and, since Mary's name did not appear and she was uncredited as the author, many people were given the mistaken impression that Shelley himself had written the work.

The book was widely read and commented on, and sometimes condemned. No less a person than Sir Walter Scott reviewed the novel in *Blackwood's Edinburgh Magazine* and he also was under the impression that Shelley was the author. He found the book had many admirable qualities: "The work impresses us with the high idea of the author's original genius and happy power of expression." But others had less regard for Mary Shelley's novel, as a critic in the March issue of *The Edinburgh Review* proved:

> When we have admitted that *Frankenstein* has passages which appal the mind and make the flesh creep, we have given it all the praise (if praise it can be called) which we dare bestow. Our taste and judgement alike revolt at

this kind of writing, and the greater the ability with which it may be executed, the worse it is.

The Monthly Review dismissed the book as worthless and thought that "a serious examination is scarcely necessary". But other publications were far more complimentary and most reviewers could not deny the novel's power to horrify. After Shelley's death Godwin wrote many letters to his daughter and in one of them he praised *Frankenstein* as "a fine thing; it was compressed, muscular and firm; nothing relaxed and weak; no proud flesh".

Mary Shelley died in 1851. In her last years she had been acknowledged as the author of *Frankenstein,* but more and more she became introverted and lived in a world where time had stood still. To her it would always be 1816, the fire would be burning brightly at the Villa Diodati while the wind whistled outside. There was talk of ghosts in the conversation of Byron and Shelley, and perhaps even of monsters.

2 The Monster Treads the Boards

Theatre audiences in the nineteenth century loved melodrama, and playwrights were constantly churning out ever more sensational fodder for their hungry customers. Plots were written and later re-vamped in an attempt to satisfy this insatiable appetite. Many playwrights sought their inspiration from novels of the day and the success of *Frankenstein* made it a suitable subject for adaptation to the stage.

Obviously there were certain problems to be overcome in the book's transition to the stage, the most important being to find the best playwright to make the adaptation. Richard Brinsley Peake was the first writer to tackle the task, and in embarking upon his adaptation of *Frankenstein*, he decided to make some fairly sweeping changes. Representing the vast panorama of the novel would not have been feasible with the average stage budget of the day, so Peake cut the scale of his work. He also had to remember that the manuscript had to pass the censor.

Peake's first task was to reorganize the characters. Some of his modifications make sense, but others are slightly puzzling. Elizabeth is now Frankenstein's sister, and Henry Clerval becomes her fiancé, while Frankenstein is in love with Agatha de Lacey, a new character. Another addition is Frankenstein's servant, Fritz, a role that reappeared in the 1931 Hollywood version of the tale. The Monster has no dialogue and his verbal utterances are limited to growls.

Peake entitled his greatly simplified version of the story *Presumption; or, The Fate of Frankenstein*, and it opened at the English Opera House on 28 July 1823. The cast included James Wallack as Frankenstein and Thomas Potter Cooke as the Monster, to which Peake referred as the Demon. When Mary Shelley returned to London she discovered that the dramatization of her novel was meeting with great success, and she eventually visited the theatre, later giving her comments on the production as well as the cast:

> But lo and behold! I found myself famous. Frankenstein had prodigious success as a drama, and was about to be repeated for the twenty-third night, at the English Opera House. The playbill amused me extremely, for, in the list of dramatis personae, came "——" by Mr T. Cooke: this nameless mode of naming the unnamable is rather good. . . .
>
> The story is well managed, but Cooke played "——" extremely well; his seeking, as it were, for support; his trying to grasp at the sounds he heard; all, indeed, he does was well imagined and executed. I was much amused and it appeared to excite a breathless eagerness in the audience.

Cooke scored a great personal success in the role of the Demon and began to become associated with the part. To many theatregoers he was the only Frankenstein Monster. Later, like other actors destined to play the role, he would grow tired of the part. Nevertheless, his contribution to the first theatrical version of *Frankenstein* was considerable.

It was common practice in the nineteenth-century theatre for managements to mount rival productions. Following closely on the heels of the English Opera House version came *Frankenstein; or The Demon of Switzerland*. This version was adapted by H. M. Milner, an even more prolific playwright than Richard Brinsley Peake, and his play opened at the Royal Coburg Theatre in London's Waterloo Road. The first night was on 18 August 1823 and gave Britain's capital the second version of Mary Shelley's story. In the same year there were also three burlesques on the Frankenstein theme.

It is sad to reflect that the success of *Frankenstein* on stage brought little financial reward to Mary Shelley, who was still attempting to find the money to educate her son. At least it can be said that the theatrical productions had fostered more interest in her literary work and therefore brought her increased sales.

T. P. Cooke was back in harness for no fewer than two productions in 1826. *Presumption; or, The Fate of Frankenstein* was revived with great success, and Cooke also appeared in a translation of a French play, *The Monster and the Magician*, by Merle and Anthony.

The following year Milner produced a new adaptation of the Frankenstein story based on the French play. It was called *The Man and the Monster* and moved even further away from Mary Shelley. Milner included a scene in which Frankenstein admits liability for the murder that his Monster has committed, the first time that Frankenstein admitted such responsibility.

The Frankenstein story was undoubtedly becoming more spectacular, but Mary Shelley's remarkable original was becoming a paler and paler shadow. In the years to come the story became even more distorted and the characters barely discernible.

Music had played an important part in the first stage versions of *Frankenstein* and indeed, there was so much music in *Presumption; or, The Fate of Frankenstein* that it had begun to verge on the operatic. On Christmas Eve 1887, London's Gaiety Theatre presented what could only be described as the first Frankenstein musical. Called *The Model Man*, it seems to have been designed as the Gaiety's Christmas pantomime and two of the theatre's most popular stars, Nellie Farren and Fred Leslie, headed

the cast. In the grand tradition of British pantomime, Miss Farren played the role of Frankenstein in the manner of a principal boy, while Fred Leslie was the latest Frankenstein creation. This was not a man pieced together from the bodies of others but an automaton. Mixed up in an incredibly involved plot were vampires, Spanish bandits, and goblins.

Fred Leslie wore a formal costume and must have been the first Frankenstein Monster to sport a monocle and bowler hat. He even sang a few songs and performed some dance routines. Somehow the creature became involved with vampires and ended up in the Arctic with one of the bloodsuckers. As a Christmas diversion allowing the Gaiety players to let their hair down, *The Model Man* could be regarded as fairly successful, but it was never deemed worthy of a revival.

In 1927 the Empire Theatre in Preston saw the première of a more conventional version of *Frankenstein* that was later restaged in 1930 at the Little Theatre in London. The guiding hand behind this production belonged to the renowned actor-manager Hamilton Deane, who had been a member of the Henry Irving Vacation Company and had even known Bram Stoker, whose *Dracula* had greatly influenced him, and he was determined to bring that extraordinary work to the stage.

Dracula opened one May evening in 1924 at the Grand Theatre in Derby. The play was a smash hit and in the years that followed it made Deane a considerable amount of money. He not only produced the play but also played the part of the vampire hunter, Van Helsing. In later years he even donned the cloak of Count Dracula himself.

Spurred on by his success with *Dracula*, Deane was on the lookout for other horror subjects and *Frankenstein* seemed the perfect follow-up to his vampire saga. Peggy Webling was responsible for the adaptation that was perhaps the most successful version of the story to appear on the stage. She was also responsible for changing Frankenstein's first name to Henry and later, when Universal came to adapt their screen version from the Webling play, they kept this innovation.

Mary Shelley would surely have approved of this version, for the Monster is treated with great sympathy. Peggy Webling also retained the Monster's wish for a bride, a wish with which Frankenstein could not comply. After destroying his creator, the creature is killed by a shaft of lightning.

Hamilton Deane played the Monster and Henry Hallat played Henry Frankenstein. Both men threw themselves into their parts with great gusto but the critics could not have cared less and gave the play a critical mauling. But Deane was unperturbed—after all, the critics had loathed his version of *Dracula* while audiences had flocked to the theatre in their hordes.

Fred Leslie as the Monster in a burlesque version of *Frankenstein* at the Gaiety Theatre, London, in 1887 (*Mander & Mitchenson Theatre Collection*)

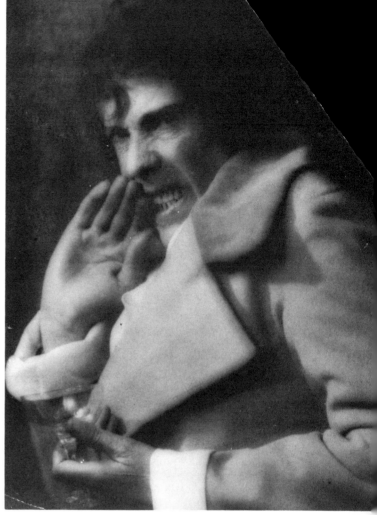

Hamilton Deane as the Monster at the Little Theatre, London, in March 1930 (*Mander & Mitchenson Theatre Collection*)

But *Frankenstein* never enjoyed the success of *Dracula* and later Deane hit upon the idea of touring provincial theatres in Britain, playing *Dracula* and *Frankenstein* on alternate nights. He thus provided a unique horror double-bill and money rolled into the box office.

Another fairly literate attempt at adaptation was made in 1936 by Miss Gladys Hastings-Walton and the resulting play was performed in Glasgow. The author attempted to stick reasonably faithfully to Mary Shelley's book, but her play did not have the pace of the Peggy Webling version. By this time, of course, the cinema had claimed the Frankenstein theme for itself and any audience visiting a stage version of the story would expect such a production to compare with its Hollywood counterparts. It is not surprising, therefore, that Frankenstein and his Monster virtually vanished from the stage.

Even Deane was forced to admit that *Frankenstein* on stage could not compete with the film industry. Hollywood had brought spectacle to the story and that could never be reproduced on stage. After seeing Universal's screen version of the story, audiences always expected too much from the stage show. The same could not be said of *Dracula*, however, for the sinister count needed fewer technical tricks and survived on stage long after he had made his screen

n Deane played the Count successfully rformance in St Helens in Lancashire e) in July 1941.

the end of the attempts to adapt ovel to the stage, however. In 1965 ental company called the Living Theatre ade an adaptation of the story that ran for between three-and-a-half and six hours. It was the work of Julian Beck and his wife Judith, and was first seen at the Bienalle Festival in Venice. The production visited Britain and eventually turned up in Chicago. Whatever the Living Theatre was attempting to say in this version, it certainly had little to do with Mary Shelley's novel, and reviewers were agreed on one aspect of the production: its inordinate length induced tedium.

Finally, mention must be made of two ingenious spoofs on the Frankenstein theme. In April 1970 the Coronet Theatre in Hollywood saw the opening night of *I'm Sorry, the Bridge is Out, You'll have to Spend the Night*. Authors Sheldon Allman and Bob Pickett united Dr Victor Frankenstein with Count Dracula, a Wolfman, and a Mummy in an affectionate look back at the standard horror film characters and clichés.

The plot begins with the old haunted house setting that has served Hollywood so well for many years. To this mansion comes a young couple in search of shelter from the storm. Needless to say, the inhabitants of the house constitute a "Who's Who" of monsterdom. Dr Frankenstein has designs on the young man's brain, which he feels would be perfect for his Monster, while the Mummy's master wishes to sacrifice the girl to the god Amon-Ra. But the villains' plans are thwarted by an alliance between the Mummy and the Monster, who put an end to the other creatures.

However, the ultimate satirical comment on the Frankenstein myth and the Universal horror film did not appear until 1973. The Classic Cinema in Chelsea, which had itself seen revivals of the Boris Karloff films, was converted into a theatre and became the home of *The Rocky Horror Show*, the brainchild of actor Richard O'Brien. Jim Sharman, the director of *Jesus Christ Superstar*, joined forces with O'Brien to produce *The Rocky Horror Show*, for both men had a love of old horror films and great respect for the conventions of the genre.

The show opened at the Theatre Upstairs, an off-shoot of London's Royal Court Theatre, and later transferred to the re-vamped Classic Cinema in Chelsea, which now became known as the King's Road Theatre. The cast was headed by a talented young actor, Tim Curry, who had also appeared in the London production of *Hair*. O'Brien not only wrote the book, music, and lyrics of the show, but also appeared as the hunchback, Riff Raff. The basic setting and opening of the production were similar to *I'm Sorry, the Bridge is Out, You'll have to Spend the Night*, but from there on the plot went deliriously wild.

Brad and Janet are a young couple who are forced to spend the night at Frank N. Furter Hall, an old, dark house with the usual assortment of strange characters. None is stranger than the owner, Frank N. Furter, a transvestite scientist who specializes in the kind of experimentation that would have gladdened the heart of Frankenstein himself. Frank's creation turns out to be a muscleman called Rocky.

The whole production was assembled with loving care. It was a tribute to Universal Pictures, a whole generation of "B" movies, and the great horror stars of the past. But it was more than just a parody, for it existed as an entity in its own right. The music was exciting and was aided by some fine lyrics. The show appeared in London at a time when the musical theatre was in the doldrums, with managements offering audiences an unvarying diet of revivals of well-known favourites. *The Rocky Horror Show* was original and audiences and critics alike lapped it up.

The theatre critic of *Punch* enthused about the cast—"No performance is less than excellent"—and was particularly impressed by Tim Curry as Frank N. Furter.

The Rocky Horror Show was a great financial success and later transferred to Broadway, with Tim Curry recreating his original role. The show continued to run in London and in 1975 Jim Sharman brought the production to the screen as *The Rocky Horror Picture Show*. The film did not diminish the audience for the stage show, and in 1979 it moved to the West End to take up residence at the Comedy Theatre where it seems set to continue its successful run.

It must be admitted that the theatre does not appear to be the most ideal medium for *Frankenstein*. The plays that were based on the book, although successful in the last century, could never be judged by today's standards, and although *Dracula* enjoyed a remarkable revival on Broadway and in London in the 1970s, no one has made a similar attempt to revive *Frankenstein*. Mary Shelley's creation was to find a happier home on celluloid and a lengthy chapter in the Frankenstein story was about to begin.

3 The Silent Monster and his Friends

On the evening of 27 December 1895 Louis and Auguste Lumière unveiled to an incredulous audience an invention that could turn fantasies into realities. In the Indian Salon of the Grand Café in the Boulevard des Capucines, a group of Parisians were treated to a short programme supplied by the new cinematograph.

The subject matter of the material featured in this first screening was far from exciting—a single shot of a train arriving at a station—but the potential of the new invention appeared limitless, and on that winter night the audience was spellbound.

Sitting in the audience was one of France's leading magicians, Georges Méliès, who saw in this first screening a potential entertainment industry. He acquired a camera and set about experimenting with the new medium. At first he simply placed his camera in front of a suitable subject and started cranking. But one day his camera jammed, then a few seconds later the fault rectified itself and the filming continued. However, when he came to view his processed print he discovered that a bus had turned into a hearse! This discovery provided Méliès with a story-telling medium with an unrivalled ability to create dreams. Special-effects photography was born.

With the help of a specially built studio, Méliès produced a whole range of cinematic fantasies and created a number of intriguing novelty shorts in which he experimented with all kinds of cinematic tricks. By 1902 he had completed the first adaptation of a Jules Verne classic when he presented *A Trip to the Moon*, and he went on to provide audiences with further fantasies, becoming so successful that his films were screened in America. But now other companies were entering the race.

By 1908 the Selig Polyscope Company had produced a version of Robert Louis Stevenson's classic *Dr Jekyll and Mr Hyde*, and entering the field with an impressive array of subjects was the Edison Company. In fact, the Edison and Biograph Companies gradually squeezed Méliès out of the American market, using the master's innovations against him until a whole new range of fantasy films brought about his bankruptcy.

Edison assembled a repertory company of actors who appeared in a wide variety of productions, and in 1910 the company embarked on their most ambitious fantasy, an adaptation of Mary Shelley's *Frankenstein*. So it was that Charles Ogle became the first actor to play the Monster on the screen, his make-up and costume making him look like a cross between a court jester and the Hunchback of Notre Dame.

Reviews were favourable and the production received much praise. Critics of the time remarked on the film's special effects and were particularly impressed by the Monster's creation in a cauldron of chemicals. In this version, directed by J. Searle Dawley, the Monster becomes jealous of Frankenstein's fiancée. The finale of the film must be the most unusual of any film in the series: the Monster is not destroyed by an act of violence but by the fact that Frankenstein's love for his fiancée is pure. The creature is sapped of its energy and literally fades away. The final title reads: "The creation of an evil mind is overcome by love and disappears."

Unfortunately no prints of this first Frankenstein film appear to be extant: it has joined the ranks of lost films. However, now and again someone unearths a print of a lost masterpiece, and many film historians live in hopes of unearthing Edison's *Frankenstein*. All that remains of the film is an exhibitor's handout and a photograph of Ogle in his Monster make-up. The Edison Company never followed up with a sequel, but there were others who were willing to try their hand at the Frankenstein myth.

The Ocean Film Corporation of New York produced *Life Without Soul*, a five-reel version of the story directed by Joseph W. Smiley. This was the first time that a Frankenstein film was made on location, as Smiley took his cast to parts of Georgia, Florida, Arizona, and even to the Atlantic on a steamship. The players included William Cohill as Frankenstein and Percy Darell Standing as the Monster. The film evidently took a more sympathetic view of the Monster and was well received by audience and press alike. Some reviewers found the location work very impressive. The film followed the fashion of the day by adding a postscript to explain to the audience that the story had merely been a dream of the hero. Producers seemed to feel the need to reassure people that cinematic fantasy was *fantasy*. Alas, once again, it is difficult to assess the quality of the production as prints no longer exist.

Another lost Frankenstein is the 1920 Italian production *Il Monstro di Frankenstein*, directed by Eugenio Testa and starring Luciano Albertini as the scientist and Umberto Guarracino as the Monster. Not even a complete plot outline of this film appears to remain. The lost *Frankensteins* remain a fascinating enigma. It can only be hoped that one day prints may be discovered and that we may glimpse some of the Monster's first cinematic movements.

There then followed a long break in the production of Frankenstein films, but the Frankenstein theme

was still present in other silent productions. During World War I and the early nineteen-twenties the German cinema was particularly oriented towards occult and fantasy subjects, and fine craftsmen were evolving a new cinematic language.

In 1914 Paul Wegener, an actor and director, had been fascinated by a legend he discovered in the city of Prague. It concerned the Golem, a clay statue built by Rabbi Judah Low Ben Bezalel to protect the Jewish community of Prague from persecution. Together with screenwriter Henrik Galeen, Wegener took the legend and fashioned it into a new story.

The film begins with the discovery of the Golem (played by Wegener himself) in the ruins of a synagogue. The statue is sold to a dealer who animates it with the help of some cabalistic texts. But the Golem must be brought to life only to protect the community, otherwise it will cease to work as a force for good, and, of course, the Golem goes on the rampage until it meets a fitting cinematic end by falling from a tower.

Der Golem was so successful that the giant man of stone was brought back in 1917 for *Der Golem und*

The only still that remains of Charles Ogle as the cinema's very first Frankenstein Monster *(Edison)*

die Tanzerin. This latter film is now feared lost for ever, and only an incomplete version of *Der Golem* has been located together with a handful of production stills.

World War I did nothing to dampen the German love of the cinema and the film industry thrived. Serials were extremely popular, and in 1916 director Otto Rippert produced *Homunculus*, a six-hour story in six chapters. A Danish matinée idol, Olaf Fonss, played an artificially created man who was not only endowed with super powers but with a formidable intellect as well.

Homunculus did not have an horrific appearance and chose to dress in black. He eventually takes over a whole country and becomes a dictator, but this bores him and he decides to lead a revolution against himself, which he then quashes. It seems that no one has the power to put an end to this monstrous creation, but Mother Nature is a force to be reckoned with and destroys him with a bolt of lightning.

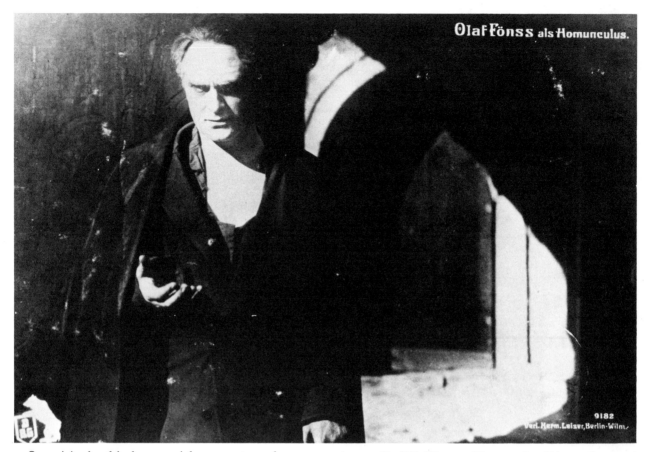

9182
Verl. Herm. Leiser, Berlin-Wilm.

A rare still of Olaf Fonss as Homunculus *(Bioscop Germany)*

Surprisingly this long serial was extremely successful. But with the end of the war the German film industry was at the crossroads, and it was in an atmosphere of political and artistic turmoil that *The Cabinet of Dr Caligari* was made. The film was the product of two young writers, Hans Janowitz and Carl Mayer, who had been inspired by the films of Paul Wegener. They created the story of a hypnotist, Dr Caligari, whose travelling sideshow conceals Cesare, a somnambulist who is under Caligari's control. The Doctor uses his slave to commit murder, but when Cesare is told to kill a beautiful girl he is unable to perform the deed and carries the girl off, only to be chased by a crowd. In the process the somnambulist dies and Caligari is unmasked and carried off in a strait-jacket.

Janowitz and Mayer had planned that the story would end there, but they had bargained without their director. Originally the producer, Erich Pommer, had attempted to gain the services of the great Austrian film-maker Fritz Lang, but Lang had other commitments and suggested Robert Wiene, who accepted. Much to the authors' annoyance, however, Wiene decided to add a prologue and an epilogue that showed that the hero of the film, who was telling the story, was, in reality, the inmate of an asylum and that the doctor in charge of the institution was Caligari himself. It all appeared to be the product of a madman's ramblings. But there was a final shot of a smiling Caligari that created a nice sense of unease.

The Cabinet of Dr Caligari not only became a classic of the cinema, but also gave a whole new lease of life to the German film industry and the fantasy film. The film was also notable for its impressionistic sets by Hermann Warm and Walter Rohrig, which gave the film a dream-like quality. In fact the choice of the décor was forced upon the producer by a more mundane factor: the simple sets were relatively cheap.

The cast included such distinguished players as Werner Krauss as Caligari and Conrad Veidt as Cesare. The somnambulist, like Frankenstein's Monster and the Golem, had a weakness for beauty, and he was sympathetically played by Veidt. The film still has the power to hold even a modern audience and its eerie quality has rarely been equalled. And it remains unique. Wiene himself attempted to use the same techniques in another film, *Genuine*, and came unstuck. There could never be another Caligari.

Paul Wegener was back in 1920 with a remake of *Der Golem*. Since the first film Wegener had become a fairly sophisticated film-maker and he now set out to improve on his original production. Hans Poelzig designed new and elaborate sets out of which Wegener rang as much atmosphere as possible.

In this new version of the legend, Rabbi Low, played by Albert Steinruck, brought the stone giant to life. Wegener once again played the Golem and was an imposing presence. His face, like that of Karloff's Frankenstein Monster, was able to evoke sympathy and pity, Perhaps the finest sequence in the film is when the stone giant, following a murder spree, comes face

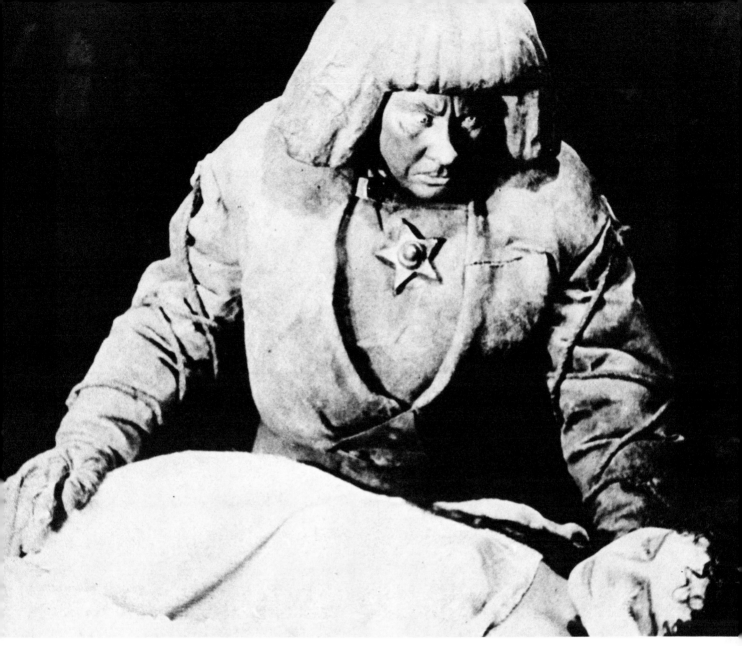

In the 1920 version of *Der Golem* Paul Wegener bends over Lyda Salmonova *(UFA)*

opposite left : Conrad Veidt is chased by a crowd after abducting Lil Dagover in *The Cabinet of Dr Caligari* *(Decla-Bioscop)*

to face with a small child who offers him an apple. The child removes the Star of David from the Golem and the giant collapses to the ground, returning to lifeless stone.

The elaborate trick photography used in the film was the work of Carl Boese, who shared directorial credit with Wegener. The legend was committed to film again in later years, but no one bettered Wegener's realization.

Such films as *The Cabinet of Dr Caligari*, *Der Golem* and *Homunculus* had a great effect on the American Frankenstein films of the thirties and forties, but one other production had an important influence on the first sound version of *Frankenstein*.

In 1926 Fritz Lang directed *Metropolis*, a dramatic vision of the future in a highly mechanized world. In one sequence, an evil scientist, Rotwang, brings to life a robot that he plans to use in the same way that Caligari used Cesare. The electrical birth of the robot inspired James Whale when he came to direct his first version of the Frankenstein myth.

The post-war German cinema had a great effect on Hollywood in the twenties and thirties, many German film-makers leaving to work in America where they stamped their own individual mark on many classic films. Universal owed a debt of gratitude to German cinema for its pioneering efforts and the European influence was to be evident in the years to come, forming an intrinsic element in the Frankenstein saga.

An exciting and stimulating era of film making was drawing to a close. Alas, many great productions will never be seen again as prints have decayed and negatives vanished. However, we are fortunate in still being able to view such masterpieces as *The Cabinet*

Paul Wegener meets a small girl in the 1920 version of the German production of *Der Golem (UFA)*

of *Dr Caligari*, the 1920 version of *Der Golem*, and Lang's incomparable *Metropolis*. May we hope that in some forgotten attic may lurk such treasures as Edison's *Frankenstein*, Smiley's *Life Without Soul*, and Wegener's early Golem productions. Such hopes now rest with film researchers and historians as we continue our progress to the American fantasy cinema of the thirties.

right : The female robot of *Metropolis (UFA)*

4 The Universal Years

In the late twenties the cinema found its voice. But the coming of sound took its toll on many a reputation, for although some actors found a new lease of life, others were consigned to the celluloid vaults. One star who found no problems in this cinematic revolution was Lon Chaney, the man of a thousand faces. Indeed he proved that he was also an excellent mimic.

In 1930 MGM remade Chaney's silent classic *The Unholy Three* and during the filming of this production the word went out that the star was likely to have an even more successful career in the sound cinema. Chaney, excited by the prospects of sound, was already looking around for a new assignment for his talents and he tentatively agreed to appear in a new production for Universal Studios.

But not long after completing *The Unholy Three* Chaney died, a victim of throat cancer. He had been about to embark upon a screen adaptation of Bram Stoker's *Dracula*, which Universal had seen as a vehicle for Chaney's talents. With the loss of their star, the studio set out to find a replacement and settled on the Hungarian actor, Bela Lugosi, who had played the role on stage for three years. Tod Browning, one of Chaney's favourite directors, took charge of the project, and a new wave of horror was born.

On St Valentine's Day 1931 Universal released the film and sat back to await results. The studio very soon realized that it had unleashed a box office bonanza; queues began to form all over America, and by the end of 1931 *Dracula* had become Universal's biggest success of the year.

Viewed today it is difficult to see what audiences found so frightening. Lugosi's performance is highly melodramatic and his style is matched by the rest of the cast. The special effects are crude by modern standards, and the scene in which David Manners chases an obviously artificial bat never fails to bring howls of laughter from a modern audience. Count Dracula's death, which should have been the high spot of the film, takes place off screen and all the audience is treated to is a scream from Lugosi. In fact, the film represents both the best and worst aspects of the early sound cinema.

The atmosphere of Count Dracula's eerie castle is beautifully evoked by some magnificently designed sets and some brooding photography. Lugosi's first appearance is highly sinister and his performance

matches the setting. But when the film moves its location to England, the dialogue becomes stilted with acting to match, while the settings are weak and the atmosphere is all but destroyed. The film gradually becomes little more than the filmed record of a play. But in 1931 it certainly exerted a power over its audiences.

Universal had had a distinguished record in the cinematic world of the supernatural. In the twenties it had produced such classics as *The Phantom of the Opera*, *The Cat and the Canary*, and *The Hunchback of Notre Dame*, and even before the completion of *Dracula* the studio was lining up the next production for its new star, Bela Lugosi. If he could play the vampiric Count Dracula Universal reasoned, he could tackle any monster and the studio earmarked him for its next excursion into the unknown—*Frankenstein*.

However, Carl Laemmle Jr had not only inherited his father's studio, he had also inherited his European caution, and he demanded a screen test of Lugosi in full make-up. A French director, Robert Florey, had been assigned to the project and, while developing the story for the screen, he shot Lugosi's test. Jack Pierce, Universal's make-up genius, set out to perfect a make-up and used as his inspiration Paul Wegener's appearance as the Golem. But he had a problem on his hands, Lugosi could not stand endless hours in the make-up chair, and the result was a patch-work creation that no one at Universal found satisfactory and some found downright hilarious.

Lugosi, who had little sympathy for the role anyway, backed out of the project, claiming that he did not accept non-speaking roles, although in the years to come he disproved that statement when he made a disastrous appearance as the Monster. The project appeared to be collapsing when an English director, James Whale, appeared on the scene. Whale had already been responsible for two big Hollywood successes, *Journey's End* and *Waterloo Bridge*, and Laemmle, who admired and respected him, was ready to offer him the project of his choice. To everyone's surprise Whale elected to film *Frankenstein*. It was a challenge to tackle a subject that many people in the industry believed to be a cinematic impossibility.

Whale's second talent was that of the casting director and he determined from the outset to select his own players. Leslie Howard was the studio's choice for Dr Frankenstein, but Whale preferred an actor with whom he had already worked, Colin Clive. Mae Clark, who had also worked with Whale, became Frankenstein's bride-to-be, Elizabeth, in preference to a young contract player called Bette Davis.

Lon Chaney, the actor who would probably have played Dracula and the Frankenstein Monster had he not met with a premature death. From *The Black Bird* *(MGM)*

But the success or failure of the film rested on the audience's acceptance of the Monster, and, as yet, there was no one to play the crucial role. Like all good Hollywood stories, however, there had to be a happy ending: if stars could be picked out of a chorus line, then monsters could be discovered in a canteen.

An English actor, who had played only modest roles in his previous films, was eating a meal at Universal when Whale saw the potential in his face. So it was that William Pratt came to sit in the make-up chair of Jack Pierce. Together Pierce and Pratt, who changed his name to Boris Karloff, worked for three weeks to perfect a make-up that was to become a classic screen creation. Pierce used his influence at the studio to delay deadlines until he was totally satisfied with the finished product. Lugosi's appearance as the Monster had been a fiasco and Pierce was not going to make the same mistake again.

Pierce put himself in Frankenstein's position and did extensive research into how the scientist would have assembled the Monster. He discovered that there were six ways in which a surgeon could cut a skull open and created a Monster with a hinged skull, held in place by clamps. The forehead betrayed more of Frankenstein's basic knowledge of surgery, while the deathly appearance of Karloff's skin was the result of make-up built up from layers of cheesecloth. False eyelids added to the creature's unearthly menace. The bolts through the neck were not, as many supposed, to hold the head on, but were intended as electrical terminals.

James Whale had also drawn some preliminary sketches and offered advice on the creation of the Monster. But the final make-up benefited from one important factor: the man wearing it knew how to use it and realized that it was possible to use his appearance to accentuate the pathos in the role.

Karloff's costume was designed to make his body look larger than it was. The sleeves on his jacket were shortened and his legs were stiffened by the use of steel braces and two pairs of trousers. His feet were encased in asphalt-spreader's boots complete with four-inch soles.

After lengthy make-up tests in front of the camera, Karloff's appearance was finally approved by Universal. The colour of the skin had been a stumbling block, but this had been finally overcome by applying a greenish-grey base. The only major modification had been the removal of the forehead scar. But now that Universal had their Monster they proposed to keep him under wraps. A blanket of security settled over the benign Karloff. Press photographs were banned and he was forced to spend his off-set moments in seclusion. It was all a magnificent publicity exercise.

The filming took place in the heat of the mid-summer. There was no air-conditioning and Karloff, all seven-and-a-half feet of him, began to suffer for his art. The perspiration made his make-up unstable, and Jack Pierce was constantly at his side to perform running repairs. Slivers of highly inflammable make-up were frequently falling into Karloff's eyes, causing him extreme discomfort. In future outings as the Monster his agony did not decrease. However, at the age of 42 he became a star.

When the film was finally released Universal had another hit on its hands. If *Dracula* had ushered in a new horror cycle, then *Frankenstein* was undoubtedly its first classic.

The film opens with an address to the audience by Edward Van Sloan, who plays Frankenstein's former tutor Dr Waldman. This had been inserted on the express orders of studio boss Carl Laemmle who felt that audiences should be warned of the horrors to come. Van Sloan obviously relished giving such a warning:

> It is one of the strangest stories ever told. It deals with the two great mysteries of creation, life and death. I think it will thrill you. It may even shock you. It might even horrify you.

Following this message we find ourselves in a grave-yard, where a newly dug grave is being looted by Dr Frankenstein and his hunchbacked assistant, Fritz. Here Whale's camera weaves its way through Herman Rosse's magnificent set, creating menace from every shadow. Already the atmosphere has been set. Then we are taken to the Frankenstein laboratory, housed in a deserted watchtower, where Frankenstein's researches are about to reach fruition. Fritz, having been sent to steal a brain from the local university, returns with a criminal's brain, but he fails to inform his master of this rather important fact and Frankenstein proceeds to insert the brain into the Monster's skull. A storm conveniently rages outside providing the life-giving force for the creature. But, just as the experiment is about to get under way, Frankenstein's fiancée together with his friend Victor and his former tutor Dr Waldman arrive on the scene to attempt to discover what the scientist is up to.

Science has moved on apace since the days of Mary Shelley, and Frankenstein explains to his tutor the process by which he will animate the lifeless body:

> I learned a great deal from you at the University—about the violet ray, the ultra-violet ray, which you said was the highest colour in the spectrum. You were wrong. Here in this machinery I have gone beyond that. I have discovered the great ray that first brought life into the world.

And sure enough, with the help of a spectacular electrical display, masterminded by special-effects wizard Ken Strickfaden, the Monster comes to life. But Frankenstein finds difficulty in controlling his creation, which later kills Fritz, who had sadistically tormented the creature. Frankenstein himself is attacked but saved by Dr Waldman, who succeeds in anaesthetizing the Monster and persuades Frankenstein to let him dissect the Monster. Alone in the operating theatre Walman is preparing for his first incision when the Monster's hand reaches up and throttles him.

Boris Karloff

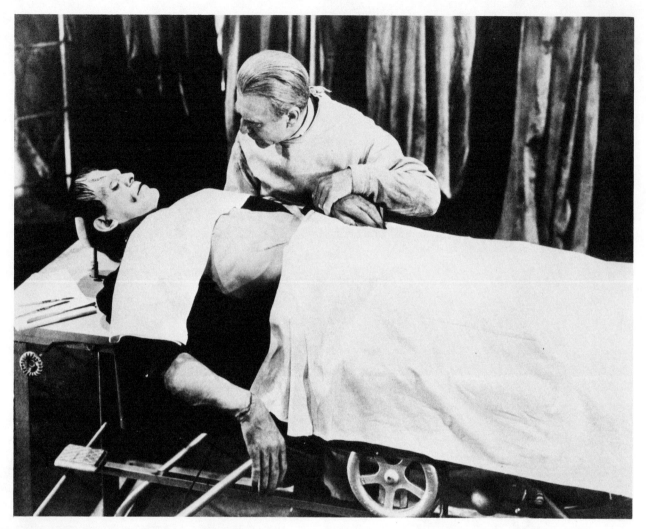

The Monster is on the loose and, after killing a small girl and attempting unsuccessfully to abduct Frankenstein's bride, he is tracked down by Frankenstein and a pack of villagers to a deserted windmill where Monster and scientist are locked in battle. The Monster throws his creator from the top of the windmill and the villagers set light to the building. As the flames climb higher the Monster is consumed by the furnace.

It was not the film of Mary Shelley's novel—that has still to be made—but somehow James Whale's production managed to capture the essence of the book. The plot had been updated to the present day, but was none the worse for that, and for some strange reason Frankenstein's first name had been changed to Henry, but he was as zealous in his pursuit of knowledge as Mary Shelley's scientist had been.

Karloff's first appearance was nicely judged. A door opens and suddenly we realize that we are looking at the back of the creature's head. Slowly he turns to reveal his face, producing not just shock, but a whole range of emotions including pity.

The acting, for the most part, is still acceptable, although Colin Clive does appear to go over the top a few times. The sets, aided by Arthur Edison's superb photography, are magnificently realized, and

Dr Waldman (Edward Van Sloan) prepares to dismember the Monster in *Frankenstein* (*Universal Pictures*)

the laboratory is a riot of electronic paraphernalia. Whale directs with a sure hand and even manages to inject some humour into the proceedings.

Universal Studios were not above a few economies. The main street of the town, a beautifully designed exterior, had recently been built for another of the company's productions, *All Quiet on the Western Front*, and would see further service in other films. Much time and finance had been expended on Frankenstein's laboratory, and that too would be pressed into service yet again in such unlikely places as the *Flash Gordon* serials.

The front office at Universal also exerted some influence over the finished film and demanded that a happy ending be added to show that Frankenstein had not been killed by his fall from the windmill. There was also one less acceptable change.

One of the film's finest scenes showed a meeting between the Monster and a small girl, the only person to treat the Monster as a normal human being. He kneels down and helps her to throw flowers into a lake. He sees the flowers floating on the water and, having

opposite right: The Monster makes his first appearance in James Whale's *Frankenstein* (*Universal Pictures*)

310-1-

no more flowers to throw in, he throws in the girl expecting that she will float as well. But a censorship cut was made that results in the scene ending when Karloff discovers that he has no more flowers left and looks at his empty hands. The next time we see the child her dead body is being carried through the streets by her father. This ridiculous cut merely implies that a far worse crime has been committed. The prints now released to television have, alas, not restored the missing footage.

Frankenstein was acclaimed by press and public alike and has earned Universal more than $12 million. As the box office takings mounted up, a sequel was surely called for, but it was not until 1935 that a second film appeared. In the meantime Karloff was contracted to Universal and although he appeared in other weird roles, sooner or later he had to return to his finest creation.

At the end of the original film the Monster had been consigned to the flames, but the front office demanded his resurrection. John L. Balderston and William Hurlbut therefore put their heads together to concoct a whole new story. The budget was increased and James Whale returned to direct the production. New characters were introduced and a team of fine character actors assembled.

The Bride of Frankenstein opens badly with Lord Byron, no less, encouraging Mary Shelley to continue her unearthly tale, but once this appalling scene is over, we settle back to enjoy another classic. The Monster, it appears, did not die in the burning windmill but fell into a pool beneath the building. After killing another villager, he heads for the woods where he finds a blind hermit who treats the Monster as a mute human being and teaches him to speak a few words. But the villagers are soon hot on the creature's tail. He is discovered by two hunters, one of whom is a very young John Carradine, and once again he is on the run.

Meanwhile Henry Frankenstein, recovering from his fall, is visited by Dr Pretorious, a scientist who is engaged on the same work as his younger rival but who has been able to produce only miniature people, whom he keeps in glass cases. He seeks Frankenstein's help in further experiments but Henry has had enough and refuses. Pretorious finds the Monster hiding in a tomb and feeds him, even offering him a glass of gin. However, Pretorious still needs Frankenstein's skill and kidnaps the scientist's wife, now played by Valerie Hobson, to force Frankenstein to help him to create a mate for the Monster and so produce a race of creatures.

Coerced into this unholy alliance, Frankenstein helps in the creation of a bride for the Monster. There have been few innovations in laboratory equipment since the earlier film, but there is an ingenious use of two huge kites to catch electricity, and another of those obliging storms allows the new creature to be animated. She is a startling creation with a mammoth shock of hair on her head, but alas, the happy couple do not hit if off, and when the bride sees the Monster she screams at him. The Monster pushes Frankenstein and his wife out of the laboratory and destroys the building together with his mate and Dr Pretorious after uttering the words "We belong dead".

The Bride of Frankenstein is considered by many to be the finest horror film ever produced and its success is in no small measure due to its splendid cast. Colin Clive and Boris Karloff were retained from the previous film, while Dwight Frye, who had played the unfortunate Fritz, was now seen as one of Dr Pretorious' assistants. Elsa Lanchester, the wife of Charles Laughton, played both Mary Shelley and the female Monster, and there was a unique line in villainy from Ernest Thesiger as Dr Pretorious, who even managed to incorporate a line he had used in a previous thriller, *The Old Dark House*, when he told the Monster that gin is "My only weakness". Mention should also be made of Una O'Connor, who graced many a fine Hollywood film and who gave another of her hilarious performances here. All in all, the film was raised to its heights by a masterly collection of talents.

Once again Universal's technical departments had excelled: Dr Pretorious and his collection of tiny people, which included an amorous Henry VIII, were painstakingly realized, and the creation of the new Monster was a fine achievement.

Karloff surpassed himself, despite sustaining a broken hip early in the shooting, but he was not happy over one matter. Whale had demanded that the Monster should speak a few lines of dialogue and Karloff disagreed completely. He thought that it made the Monster a laughing stock. In fact the success or failure of the film relies on the audience's acceptance of Whale's black sense of humour, but, as it happened, the Monster had spoken virtually his last words, for in the climax of *The Ghost of Frankenstein* his speech would return, but only briefly.

Through the passage of the years the film's reputation has increased and many enthusiasts believe it to be that rare cinematic animal—the sequel that is superior to its original. There is also no doubt that *The Bride of Frankenstein* stands the test of time extremely well and is perhaps the finest horror film of the thirties.

And still the money flowed into the box office. And still Universal had not learned to refrain from killing off such a profitable creation. Another writer was soon to be called upon to find a way of exhuming him from the ashes.

In January 1939 *Son of Frankenstein* appeared. The times were changing, but the Monster was as lethal as ever. Wolf von Frankenstein, with his wife and son, arrives from America to claim the inheritance of his father's estate to a decidedly chilly reception. The

opposite above : A rare shot of director James Whale dusting down Boris Karloff on the set of *The Bride of Frankenstein (Universal Pictures)*

opposite : The Monster (Boris Karloff) meets his bride (Elsa Lanchester) in *The Bride of Frankenstein (Universal Pictures)*

above : Henry Frankenstein (Colin Clive) and Dr Pretorious (Ernest Thesiger) examine the female Monster (Elsa Lanchester) in *The Bride of Frankenstein (Universal Pictures)*

right : Henry Frankenstein (Colin Clive) and his new Monster (Elsa Lanchester) in *The Bride of Frankenstein (Universal Pictures)*

opposite left : One of the great character actresses of the thirties, Una O'Connor, is confronted with the Monster (Boris Karloff) in *The Bride of Frankenstein (Universal Pictures)*

MONSTER WORLD

MARCH NO. 7

35¢
PDC

SPECIAL BONUS THIS ISSUE:
"SON OF FRANKENSTEIN"
COMPLETE WITH RARE PICTURES!!

local Burgomaster hands Wolf a box of papers that contains his father's notes on his experiments and a note begging him to carry on the pioneering work. Wolf decides that he will succeed where his father failed.

But all is not well with the local villagers. Inspector Krogh, the local police chief, advises Frankenstein that he and his family should leave for their own safety, adding that there have been a number of unexplained murders. But Frankenstein laughs off the suggestion that the Monster is on the loose again. However Krogh has bitter memories of his own childhood experience: "One doesn't easily forget, Herr Baron, an arm torn out by the roots."

Wolf decides to explore the remains of his father's laboratory and discovers a bubbling sulphur pit in the ruins (the building had originally been built over the remains of a Roman health spa!). He also meets a strange character called Ygor, a convicted murderer who had been hanged and left for dead, but who in fact had merely been left with a broken neck. Ygor has a surprise for Wolf: he shows him the Monster.

The creature, it appears, has survived the destruction of the laboratory and has been befriended by Ygor. But at the moment the Monster is conveniently unconscious thanks to a tree having fallen on him in a storm. Wolf makes an instant diagnosis and prepares to revive the Monster.

So, once again the villagers grow uneasy as yet another batch of laboratory equipment is delivered to the Frankenstein home. Wolf assures the Inspector that he is engaged on "simple chemical research", but, with a family history like the Frankensteins', who could believe that?

With the help of Benson (the butler) and Ygor, Wolf attempts to engender life into the Monster, but when the creature finally awakens from his slumbers Frankenstein discovers that only Ygor can control him, and furthermore Ygor will agree to no more surgical tamperings.

Ygor sends the Monster to kill the foreman of the jury that convicted him, and once again the creature begins a reign of terror. Wolf attempts to solve his problems by finding Ygor, but the Monster's only friend attacks Wolf and in the struggle Ygor is killed.

When the Monster discovers that his friend is dead he is overcome by grief and bent on vengeance, kidnapping Wolf's son. He is hunted down by Inspector Krogh and in the grand finale Frankenstein saves his son by kicking the Monster into the boiling sulphur; Wolf and his family then decide to return to America.

Son of Frankenstein again demonstrated that Universal certainly knew a thing or two about casting. Karloff returned as the Monster with a brand new wardrobe, including a sheepskin wrap. Basil Rathbone, who had the previous year begun a distinguished career as Sherlock Holmes, played

opposite left: **Son of Frankenstein** is featured in another issue of Monster World *(Warren Publishing)*

Wolf von Frankenstein (the "von" had appeared out of nowhere). Lionel Atwill was not his usual sinister self when he was cast as Inspector Krogh, and Edgar Norton was a magnificently unflappable butler.

But the revelation of the film was Bela Lugosi's performance as Ygor. It was a fine piece of character acting and arguably Lugosi's finest performance, for he managed to appear sinister rather than melodramatic. Perhaps this was the high spot of Lugosi's career; within a few years his stature diminished rapidly.

For the third film in the series Universal introduced a new director. Gone was the humour of James Whale, and instead the film was entrusted to Rowland V. Lee, an ex-actor who had been directing since 1926, including such lively pieces as *The Count of Monte Cristo* and *The Three Musketeers*. He had a fine sense of style and believed in producing films with pace, but not at the expense of characterization.

The plot proved that there was still plenty of life in the Frankenstein saga. Once again, the film

Karloff receives some finishing touches to his costume in *Son of Frankenstein (Universal Pictures)*

benefited from the introduction of new characters and some fine performances, and it is quite possible to gloss over its few imperfections, such as a truly appalling performance from Donnie Dunagan as Wolf's son. It is also noticeable that the central European setting has some alarming American intrusions, such as the train that transports Wolf to his ancestral home. It had been planned to film this production in colour, but Karloff's make-up was not deemed suitable for the process.

Universal had certainly produced a fine film, but the writing was on the wall and the company had reached its zenith as far as horror was concerned. Karloff knew that from now on the Monster would become a lumbering thug, and it was the last time that he played Frankenstein's creation, apart from a television spoof in the sixties.

But the money was still rolling in and by 1942 Universal was convinced that there was a rich vein of horror still to be tapped. *Dracula* and *Frankenstein* had been issued as a double-bill to incredible success and it was clear that the Monster would have to rise again. But who would play him?

opposite : Bela Lugosi at the height of his career

Lionel Atwill, Basil Rathbone and Josephine Hutchinson in *Son of Frankenstein (Universal Pictures)*

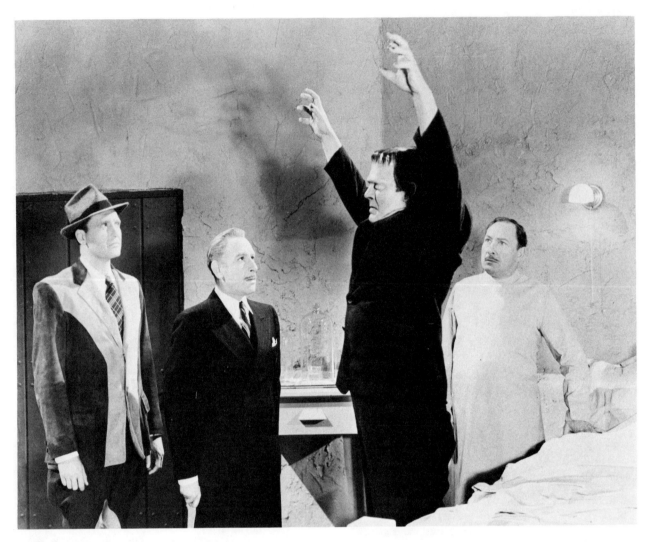

A vintage cast: Ralph Bellamy, Sir Cedric Hardwicke, Lon Chaney Jr and Lionel Atwill in *The Ghost of Frankenstein (Universal Pictures)*

An actor obviously worth grooming for greater things was Lon Chaney Jr, the son of the great silent horror star, who had appeared in the highly profitable production *The Wolf Man*. He was not a great actor, but he was an effective horror player and he now succeeded Karloff in Jack Pierce's make-up chair.

The new film, *The Ghost of Frankenstein*, showed that Universal was to turn a blind eye to the incongruities in the Frankenstein saga. Old Ygor, for example, who had been shot in the previous production, appears again, hail and hearty.

The Monster is revived by an electrical storm in an extremely impressive scene, but doesn't meet with the instant approval of Ludwig Frankenstein, the great man's other son, who wants to dismember the creature. He is prevented from doing this by his father's ghost, who explains that the Monster's fatal flaw lies in its brain. If this were replaced the experiment would be a success.

So, like the trusting son that he is, Ludwig looks around for a new brain. And what better than the brain of a former colleague, Dr Kettering. However, he has two things against him, or should we say two people. First there is Frankenstein's assistant, played by Lionel Atwill, who had previously appeared in the series as a policeman; second, there is the scheming Ygor. Together they combine to deceive Frankenstein, and after the scientist has completed the brain transplant, Ludwig is astonished to find that the brain is that of Ygor. The Monster even speaks with Ygor's voice. But, just when all seems lost, the Monster goes blind and stumbles around the laboratory as, once again, fire consumes the evil of the Frankensteins.

It was obvious that the Monster needed more than a transfusion to bring some life into the series. True, there were one or two good scenes, but really the audience had been treated to a rehash of a familiar theme. Erle C. Kenton, who had produced the imaginative *Island of Lost Souls*, was brought in to direct the proceedings and found that it was uphill going. Chaney was no Karloff and the entire production can only be described as routine. The magic flashed for no more than a moment.

right : The Monster (Lon Chaney Jr) meets a small child in *The Ghost of Frankenstein (Universal Pictures)*

Lon Chaney Jr as Lawrence Talbot, the Wolfman, who was involved in four films in the Frankenstein series (*Universal Pictures*)

Perhaps Universal sensed this and decided that it was necessary to overhaul the formula. The answer was to double the number of monsters and the following year the studio decided to produce a film that was a sequel to not one, but two productions. Chaney may not have been an outstanding success as the Frankenstein Monster, but he had been impressive in *The Wolf Man*, so the sagas were combined in *Frankenstein meets the Wolfman*. Of course, Chaney could not play both monsters, so an aging Lugosi was offered the part, and since Lugosi could no longer afford the luxury of picking and choosing his parts, he had to accept any roles that came his way. But when he was required to take part in any strenuous scenes, his place was taken by Universal stuntman Edwin Parker.

Larry Talbot has been bitten by a werewolf, and after wreaking havoc in the area was killed by his father and buried. As the new film opens we are in the Welsh town of "Llanelly", although Hollywood's idea of Wales is closer to Bavaria. Two grave-robbers attempting to loot the Talbot tomb are startled to find the body of Larry Talbot perfectly preserved, even though he has been buried for four years. But, as the full moon shines, Larry becomes a werewolf and attacks—once again the werewolf is on the loose. When he returns to his normal self, however, Larry determines to find a cure for his affliction and fate takes him to a hospital where he is unable to convince Dr Mannering, one of the consultants, that he is a werewolf. Instead, thinking that Talbot is a lunatic, Mannering has him placed in a strait-jacket, although later the doctor checks Talbot's story and discovers that Larry is telling the truth.

But, having escaped by biting through his strait-jacket, Larry once again meets the gypsy Maleva, whose son's bite had originally transformed him into a werewolf. She suggests that Dr Frankenstein may have the answer to Larry's affliction and together they head for Vassaria. But alas, at the journey's end they discover that Frankenstein is dead and hope seems lost. The full moon peeps through the clouds and Talbot once again changes into a snarling monster. Chased by the villagers he falls into an underground cave where he discovers the frozen form of Frankenstein's Monster, which, needless to say, thaws out. Dr Mannering arrives from England on Talbot's trail and, with Baroness Elsa, the last surviving member of the Frankenstein family, finds Talbot and visits the ruins of the Frankenstein castle. Mannering hopes that Frankenstein's documents will enable him to find a cure for the Wolfman, but he also hopes to see Frankenstein's Monster in all its glory. As usual things go magnificently wrong: the Monster goes beserk, Larry changes into the Wolfman, and the two monsters set about each other. Meanwhile the villagers have dynamited a dam and water consumes the castle and washes the two monsters away.

The film was an improvement on its predecessor, but it was by no means a success, for although the opening led one to expect a classic Universal horror, the promise was not fulfilled. The fault was not the director's. As his Sherlock Holmes films with Basil Rathbone show, Roy William Neill was the master of the small budget and was capable of getting the best out of a mediocre script and competent cast. However, he was not helped by some pre-release pruning that made nonsense out of a major plot detail. At the end of *The Ghost of Frankenstein* the Monster had been blind, but in the new film this was not explained because vital scenes had been removed. Lugosi experiences difficulty in walking because he cannot see where he is going. In the finale the Monster's eyelids suddenly open, he grins, and we know that his sight has been restored.

Curt Siodmak's screenplay was quite ingenious in its way, but somehow there was a sense of desperation about the proceedings. And Lugosi's Monster made one appreciate Karloff's achievement.

The series was in desperate need of new ideas and new talent, but Universal fell back on its old theory of producing more of the same but in greater quantities. After all, if Frankenstein's Monster could meet the Wolfman, why not include some more horrors along the way? Siodmak was told to write a story involving not only the Frankenstein Monster and the Wolfman, but also Count Dracula. Siodmak went one better, however, and included a mad doctor

Dr Niemann (Boris Karloff) removes a stake from Count Dracula's skeleton and the vampire (John Carradine) returns to life in House of Frankenstein (Universal Pictures)

with a hunchbacked assistant. The story was then adapted by screenwriter Edward T. Lowe into a script entitled *Chamber of Horrors*, which appeared in 1944 as *House of Frankenstein*.

Dr Gustav Niemann has been imprisoned for performing experiments along the lines of those pioneered by Dr Frankenstein. With his hunchbacked cell-mate Daniel he escapes after an earthquake has destroyed his prison. Niemann promises Daniel that he will build him a new body and together they set off to find Castle Frankenstein. On the way they come across the travelling horror show of Professor Lampini and, after disposing of him, Niemann assumes his identity.

Niemann decides to put on a show at the town of Reigelburg where, years before, he had been convicted. One of the exhibits is the skeleton of Count Dracula with a stake through its chest. After the show Niemann removes the stake and the Count reappears. The scientist offers to protect the vampire's coffin if Dracula will help him gain vengeance against the local Burgomaster. The Count agrees and kills the local official, but a vampire can never resist a pretty neck and he attempts to abduct a local girl. The police chase Dracula and Niemann throws his coffin from the caravan, abandoning the vampire to his fate. The first rays of dawn destroy the Count as he attempts to clamber into his coffin.

As they journey to Castle Frankenstein, Niemann and Daniel save a gypsy girl called Ilonka from being unjustly punished. Later, in the ruins of the castle, Niemann locates not only Frankenstein's records, but also the frozen forms of the Monster and the Wolfman. The creatures are thawed out, but although Talbot (the Wolfman) returns to his mortal shape, the Monster needs to be revived by electricity, so the party moves to Niemann's old laboratory, Talbot having been promised a cure by the scientist. To Daniel's dismay Ilonka falls in love with Talbot, who, after again turning into the Wolfman, this time killing a villager, explains his affliction and asks the girl to shoot him with a silver bullet. Ilonka is reluctant

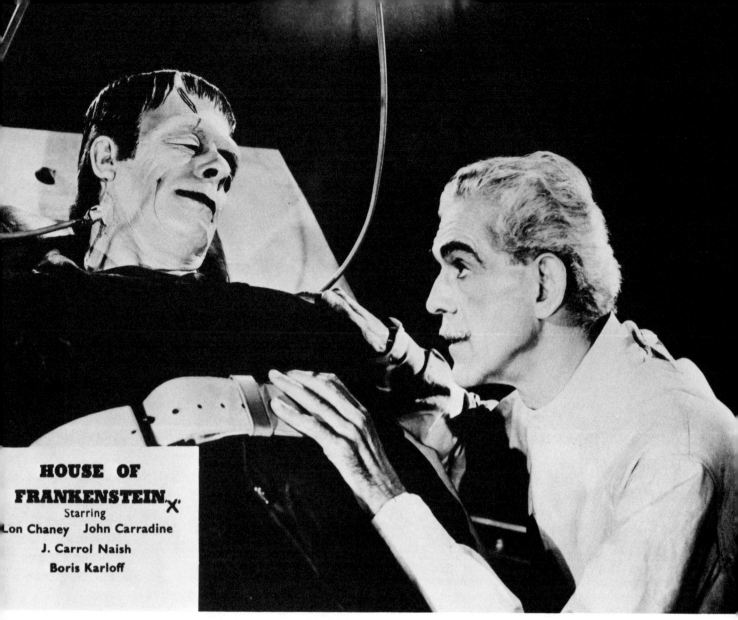

HOUSE OF
FRANKENSTEIN x
Starring
Lon Chaney   John Carradine
J. Carrol Naish
Boris Karloff

until Larry is again transformed into a werewolf and before she dies, she shoots the Wolfman.

Meanwhile Niemann has revived the Monster, who kills Daniel and then drags Niemann into a quicksand as the villagers follow in pursuit. Together the creature and the scientist disappear from sight.

Karloff had returned to the series, this time as the evil Dr Niemann, and was joined by John Carradine as Dracula and Chaney as the Wolfman. In supporting roles were Lionel Atwill and George Zucco. This distinguished company was directed by Erle C. Kenton, who also returned to the series, but the film did not add up to the sum of its parts. None of the performers was allowed sufficient chance to display his talents: Carradine's Dracula was polished off fairly quickly; Chaney's werewolf was sent on only a minor rampage; and Frankenstein's Monster did not come to life until the finale. All in all there was not much to enjoy in *House of Frankenstein*.

The fourth actor to don the Monster's make-up was Glenn Strange, who had played a number of minor roles before playing the title role in the 1941 production, *The Mad Monster*. Strange was being

Dr Niemann (Boris Karloff) continues to experiment with the Frankenstein Monster (Glenn Strange) in *House of Frankenstein (Universal Pictures)*

opposite above: Glenn Strange becomes *The Mad Monster* and George Zucco attempts to control him *(PRC)*

opposite: Dr Edelmann (Onslow Stevens) revives the Monster (Glenn Strange) in *House of Dracula (Universal Pictures)*

made-up for a supporting part in an Yvonne de Carlo film when Jack Pierce noticed his profile. Producer Paul Malvern was called in and agreed that Strange had a perfect facial structure for the Monster make-up. After a test the part was his.

Glenn Strange took the role seriously and received tuition from the master himself. Karloff showed him how to adopt the Monster's walk and how to use his appearance to its best effect. Later Strange said: "If I made a good monster, the credit goes to one of the nicest guys I know, Boris Karloff."

The Monster cycle was drawing to a close and Universal realized it. But there were still a few dollars to be drawn from the fans and the company rushed the monsters back into the *House of Dracula*. Surprisingly, this was a slight improvement on its predecessor.

By this time no one was bothering to explain the return of Count Dracula and the Wolfman after their deaths. Onslow Stevens played the kindly Dr Edelmann who appears to possess an endless fund of scientific expertise, and it is no wonder that in the same night both Count Dracula and Larry Talbot turn up on his doorstep looking for cures. Edelmann tells Dracula that his condition can be controlled by

Dr Edelmann (Onslow Stevens) is attacked by the Wolfman (Lon Chaney Jr) in *House of Dracula (Universal Pictures)*

the introduction of antibodies, and the Count agrees to submit to the treatment, which involves blood transfusions from Edelmann's own body.

Edelmann is less sympathetic to Talbot until he sees him change into the Wolfman. But once again the good doctor has the answer. He has been working to create a fungus that will soften bone and Edelmann is convinced that by thus enlarging Larry's cranium, the Wolfman's activities will be forever halted.

But all is not well. Dracula decides that he no longer wants to be cured and during the transfusion the vampire's blood is redirected into Edelmann's body so that within a short time the doctor begins to suffer periodic transformations into a crazed killer. Edelmann also discovers in a cave below his house the body of Frankenstein's Monster, clutching the skeleton of Dr Niemann. After operating on Talbot, the crazed Edelmann revives the Monster and the villagers once again go hunting. Edelmann is killed, the Monster dies in a blazing laboratory, and Talbot survives, apparently cured.

Both Carradine and Chaney returned in the roles of Dracula and the Wolfman, and Onslow Stevens made an excellent impression as Edelmann. John P. Fulton recreated an ingenious effect, originally designed for the *House of Frankenstein*, whereby Carradine changed into an animated bat, and he was also responsible for Chaney's transformation scenes. Kenton was better served by a script from Edward T. Lowe, which was a model of brevity. The pace was hectic and the running time just over an hour.

The shortcomings of the budget were evident in a finale that included footage from *The Ghost of Frankenstein*. Hence Chaney's Frankenstein Monster made an unheralded appearance from the earlier film, and some superb editing helped to blend the old shots into the new film.

If the series had ended then it would have been a kindness, but Universal had other ideas. The studio reasoned that audiences were now laughing at the monsters, so why not play them for laughs? Bud Abbott and Lou Costello were at the height of their popularity and Universal dreamed up the idea of pitting them against the monsters in *Abbott and Costello meet Frankenstein*.

Chaney was back as the Wolfman (the operation in the previous film must not have been a success), Strange played the Monster, and Lugosi returned as Count Dracula. The production was not without its troubles. Lou Costello read the script and announced:

Abbott and Costello pose with the Wolfman (Lon Chaney Jr) and the Frankenstein Monster (Glenn Strange) during the filming of *Abbott and Costello Meet Frankenstein* (*Universal Pictures*)

"It stinks." But Universal's cheque book persuaded him that he was perhaps wrong. Strange damaged his foot during filming and in one scene Chaney replaced him when the Monster was called upon to throw a girl through a window.

The plot concerned Count Dracula's attempts to find a new brain for the Frankenstein Monster. He decides that Lou Costello is the perfect donor, but his plans come unstuck and the vampire decides to escape by turning into a bat. The Wolfman leaps at the bat and both monsters plunge to a watery grave. The Frankenstein Monster met a fate that had already faced him a number of times when he was engulfed in another inferno.

Box offices throughout the world were once again busy, and Abbott and Costello continued to meet other famous fantasy characters such as the Invisible Man, Dr Jekyll and Mr Hyde, and the Mummy. Bud and Lou had managed to do what thousands of howling mobs brandishing fiery torches had only dreamed of: they had killed the Monster and his cohorts for ever. Universal turned its back on its once great creation and it was now up to other companies to revive interest in Mary Shelley's creation.

47

5 A Feast of British Blood

After Abbott and Costello had met Frankenstein, the Monster lay dormant for a number of years, but in 1952 he made a half-hearted appearance in a French production, *Torticola contre Frankensberg*, which was directed by Paul Paviot and which had the sole distinction of featuring that fine actor Michel Piccoli as the Monster. Needless to say the film failed to kindle the old Universal spirit.

But in 1957 a British company, Hammer Films, decided to gamble on there still being a market for the horror film. Hammer came into existence in 1934 with the production of a number of low-budget pictures, although in 1936 it had employed Bela Lugosi to appear in *The Mystery of the Marie Celeste* (released in America as *The Phantom Ship*). Hammer continued its policy of importing American stars (many of whom were on the wane) to ensure that its films were distributed in America. Louis Hayward, Paul Henreid, and George Brent all appeared in Hammer films.

Hammer's productions were generally thrillers, although it did occasionally branch into other genres. Some of its films originated in radio serials—*PC Forty-Nine* and *Dick Barton*, for example—but Hammer was quick to capitalize on the new medium, television, and when BBC Television came up with a spine-chilling serial called *The Quatermass Experiment*, Hammer quickly negotiated the screen rights and rushed the film version into production.

Brian Donlevy was imported to play Professor Quatermass and Hammer hooked up an American distribution deal. The film was an unqualified success and Hammer continued its output of science-fiction sagas with *X—The Unknown* and a further Quatermass film, *Quatermass II*. Then the company moved into the realms of the wide-screen with *The Abominable Snowman*, which starred an up-and-coming actor called Peter Cushing.

In 1957 Hammer decided to take its biggest gamble when it announced that it proposed to film Mary Shelley's classic as *The Curse of Frankenstein*. But Hammer was about to bring the creature to the screen in a way that he had never been seen before—in the full glory of Eastman Colour—and there were other changes that would have made Karloff's Monster turn in its grave, if it had one.

Universal had refrained from showing the gorier aspects of Frankenstein's activities, and indeed, the doctor himself had been portrayed as a dedicated,

The Monster (Glenn Strange) gets to grips with Bud and Lou when *Abbott and Costello Meet Frankenstein* (*Universal Pictures*)

but somewhat misguided, medical examiner. Peter Cushing's Baron Frankenstein was totally ruthless and thought nothing of killing off his old tutor so that he could use his brain for the Monster. The film also went into much detail over the surgical aspects of the Monster's creation: Frankenstein was seen examining human eyes in close-up, and severed limbs were also displayed before being assembled into a creature. Hammer sensibly decided to go back to a period close to that of the original novel, and in this respect was completely successful, for the modern-day trappings of the Universal series had sometimes proved jarring.

There were no imported actors, the cast being drawn from English players. Peter Cushing was an admirable and utterly believable Frankenstein, and Hazel Court was attractive and intelligent as the scientist's bride-to-be. Robert Urquhart played Frankenstein's colleague with great dignity, and was supported by some fine character actors who were seen again in later films. Some of the sets were also used in other productions.

But the success of *The Curse of Frankenstein* rested on the shoulders of the actor who played the Monster and of the make-up artist. Hammer offered the role to a tall actor who had appeared in many films but had never been a featured player. His name was Christopher Lee and, like Karloff before him, it was another case of a Monster making an actor.

The Universal make-up could not be used as it was still under copyright, so Hammer gave the task of creating a new Monster to Phil Leakey who began experimenting with Lee's features and finally came up with a creature that looked as if it had been pieced together by a madman. However, it lacked the brilliance of Jack Pierce's conception: here was a Monster who engendered total revulsion, while the Pierce make-up had given Karloff the opportunity for more pathos. But it is to Lee's credit that he made a distinctive creature and managed to achieve many spendid moments. It opened the door to a distinguished career in fantasy films.

The film was directed by Terence Fisher, who managed to achieve a style that was totally in keeping with the production. Hammer obtained prints of some of the Universal films but Fisher refused to see them. He wanted to make a film that was totally different from James Whale's style.

The Curse of Frankenstein has stood the test of time remarkably well and its moments of shock remain effective if obvious, but in its day it was condemned by nearly every critic in the land. Audiences lapped it up, however, and when prints of the film, which was

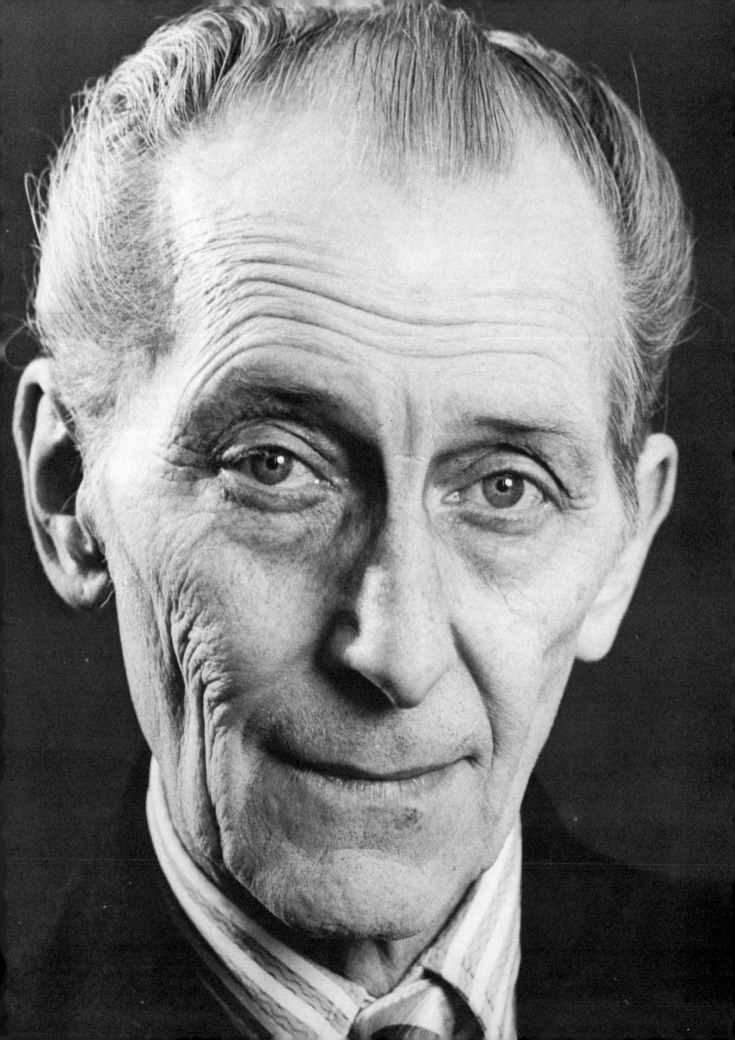

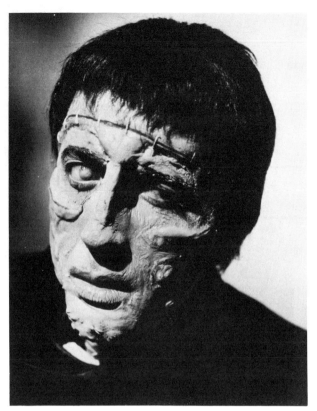

above left : Christopher Lee as the first Hammer
Frankenstein Monster; Phil Leaky was responsible for this
make-up in *The Curse of Frankenstein (Warner Brothers/
Hammer)*

above right : Christopher Lee in 1966 *(Hammer)*

opposite left : Peter Cushing – a recent photograph
(Anglia Television)

distributed by Warner Brothers, were rushed to Jack
L. Warner himself, he immediately forecast a gold-
mine in the offing.

Hammer found itself with not only a domestic hit
on its hands, but an international one as well.
Hollywood sat up and took another look at the British
company. Offers began to come from several
American distributors and Hammer decided that it
might be wise to spread its wings and deal with other
Hollywood giants as well. Universal had been much
impressed by Hammer and funded the company's
remake of *Dracula*. Columbia also paid court to
Hammer and eventually contracted them to produce
four films a year, and it was to Columbia that
Hammer offered its sequel to *The Curse of
Frankenstein*.

Hammer was now faced with the problem of how to
bring the Baron back from the grave. In the previous
film he had been convicted of committing the crimes
perpetrated by the Monster and as the final credits
rolled the guillotine had been seen to descend. But on
whose neck had it actually struck?

The Revenge of Frankenstein solved the problem by
revealing that Frankenstein had cheated the blade
with the help of Hans, a mis-shapen prison warder.
In return for his help, Frankenstein offers to build
Hans a new body and the pair end up in the town of
Carlsbruck where Frankenstein practices medicine
under the name of Dr Stein. He even opens a hospital
for the poor, but with an ulterior motive—for he
collects limbs from the patients for use in his
experiments.

Soon Frankenstein has created a new body for the
brain of Hans and, helped by his new assistant

opposite above : Robert Urquhart tries to prevent Christopher Lee from strangling Peter Cushing in *The Curse of Frankenstein (Warner Brothers/Hammer)*

above : Grave times for grave-robbers. Peter Cushing and his assistant in *The Revenge of Frankenstein (Columbia–EMI–Warner)*

opposite : Two Frankensteins for the price of one: Peter Cushing poses on the set of *The Curse of Frankenstein* with Melvyn Hayes who plays Victor as a youth *(Warner Brothers/Hammer)*

(Francis Matthews), he completes the transplant. But Hans ignores Frankenstein's advice and sets out to try his new body too soon after the operation. After being involved in a fight Hans discovers that his body is beginning to twist into its old shape. He seeks out Frankenstein and exposes him at a party. Frankenstein returns to his hospital, where he is set upon by the inmates and savagely beaten. But his assistant transplants his brain into another body, which Frankenstein had previously constructed, and the film ends with a certain Dr Frank practising medicine among London society. For the first time, Frankenstein actually becomes his own creation.

The Revenge of Frankenstein is perhaps the most interesting of Hammer's excursions into Mary Shelley's tale. Michael Gwynn's portrayal of the new creature was far removed from Christopher Lee's Monster. The atmosphere was magnificently evoked, and Jack Asher's photography and Bernard Robinson's production designs did much to enhance it. Once again Terence Fisher showed that he was a director to be reckoned with, and Hammer was to be complimented in the way it chose not to settle for a mere rehash of its previous film.

The credit for much of Hammer's success with its first two Frankenstein films must be attributed to screenwriter Jimmy Sangster, who produced his own

versions of the myth with great skill and craftsmanship. He also knew how to write for a restricted budget. The second film also proved that Sangster could create a highly successful variation on the theme.

But when Hammer came to add a third film to the series, Sangster did not provide the script; instead producer Anthony Hinds turned his hand to writing under the pen-name John Elder. *The Evil of Frankenstein* was financed by Universal and much was expected from the film. Many had supposed that Hammer would make a film whose plot was a logical continuation of *The Revenge of Frankenstein*, but the new production totally disregarded the previous films.

Frankenstein has been driven from his castle in Karlstaad after the villagers have chased his Monster into the mountains and seen him plunge to his death. But it is not long before the Baron and his assistant discover the Monster encased in ice in a cave. After thawing the creature out, the Baron finds that he is unable to revive him because his brain has been damaged. In the town Frankenstein meets Zoltan, a hypnotist, who has been hounded by the local police. Zoltan agrees to use his powers to revive the Monster and the process is a complete success. But Zoltan is out for revenge and commands the Monster to rob and kill for him. Frankenstein discovers this and confronts the hypnotist. Zoltan orders the Monster to kill Frankenstein, but the creature kills Zoltan instead. After roaming around on the loose the

Michael Gwynn as Peter Cushing's second creation makes a startling appearance at a dinner party in *The Revenge of Frankenstein (Columbia–EMI–Warner)*

Monster returns to Frankenstein's laboratory where he drinks a bottle of brandy. Frankenstein attempts to stop the creature but is unsuccessful in preventing him from drinking a bottle of chloroform. In agony the Monster staggers round the laboratory, starting a fire in the process. The castle explodes and the final credits roll.

The Evil of Frankenstein showed little invention. Instead the series had produced one of its weakest movies, no more than a collection of favourite clichés from previous films: once again villagers mumbled into their beer mugs and cursed the name of Frankenstein; the Monster was discovered frozen in a block of ice (although it was obviously polythene) as Glenn Strange had been in *House of Frankenstein*; and the creature's liking for alcohol was regrettably imported from *The Bride of Frankenstein*. In short, the film was a rehash and unworthy of the name of Frankenstein.

Kiwi Kingston, a former wrestler, played the Monster and his make-up, loosely modelled on the Jack Pierce concept, was applied by Roy Ashton who was later to produce better work in a host of Hammer films. The result was not satisfying and Kiwi Kingston was no Boris Karloff. The cast, which included such fine players as Peter Woodthorpe, Duncan Lamont, and James Maxwell, attempted to

rise to the occasion. But the script was against them.

Terence Fisher was absent from the director's chair and his place was taken by ex-cameraman Freddie Francis, who had photographed that memorable excursion into cinematic terror, *The Innocents*. Although Francis later proved a highly successful director of such films as *The Skull* and *The Creeping Flesh*, he was unable to make much out of *The Evil of Frankenstein*.

The film's only saving grace was Peter Cushing's Baron Frankenstein, whose character had been firmly stamped in the previous films. In future productions Hammer relied heavily on Cushing to create a brooding sense of menace.

When the film was sold to television, Universal, who had made a considerable profit from its theatrical release, discovered that it was too short for a major network time slot. American footage with a completely new sub-plot was added, but the extra scenes served only to demonstrate how not to tackle the Frankenstein story. It was indeed time for Hammer to reconsider its approach to the work of one of the cinema's leading scientists.

Peter Cushing creates Kiwi Kingston in *The Evil of Frankenstein (Rank/Hammer)*

By 1967 Hammer had decided to bring back the Baron for a fourth film. This time there was to be no Monster. John Elder had decided that Frankenstein should move with the times and the new production concentrated on the Baron's surgical skill. It was also aimed at an increasingly more permissive audience and was saddled with the title *Frankenstein Created Woman*. From now on sex was to play a greater part in Hammer Films.

Baron Frankenstein seemed none the worse for his experiences in the fiery climax to the previous film, although he was now unable to perform surgical operations after suffering damage to his hands. However, a new colleague, Dr Hertz, performs the various surgical manoeuvres under Frankenstein's instruction.

Heart transplants and other surgical breakthroughs were making headlines in the mid-sixties, and the Baron was forced to move with the times. He had even managed to present an innovation of his own, a

above: Christina (Susan Denberg), after her transformation by Baron Frankenstein, sets off on a murder spree as she eyes up another victim (Barry Warren) in *Frankenstein Created Woman* (Columbia–EMI–Warner)

below: Peter Cushing surveys his latest experiment in the shape of Susan Denberg in *Frankenstein Created Woman* (Columbia–EMI–Warner)

soul transplant. It was at least an original idea, but it didn't measure up to its initial promise.

Baron Frankenstein, with the help of Dr Hertz and his assistant Hans, is engaged in an experiment to prove that the soul survives the body after death. The local inn-keeper's crippled daughter, Christina, is taunted by three village youths, and Hans intervenes on her behalf. The youths attack Christina's father and Hans finds himself accused of murder. Frankenstein is unable to save Hans from the guillotine but, being the great scientist he is, the Baron collects Hans' body and returns it to his laboratory. Christina, who has witnessed the execution, throws herself into a river. Her body also finds its way to Frankenstein's laboratory. The Baron brings Christina back to life and removes the deformities from her body, at the same time transferring the soul of Hans to his girlfriend's body. However this latest creation now begins a spree of vengeance and Christina eventually kills all three of the youths before committing suicide. Frankenstein is left to bemoan another unsuccessful experiment.

Those who were lured into the cinema by the catchpenny title probably felt cheated by the loss of a conventional Monster and many people had expected that the new film would be fashioned along the lines of *The Bride of Frankenstein*. Instead Hammer concentrated on a series of outlandish murders. Terence Fisher had returned to the series and certainly the production had a more assured look and was an improvement on *The Evil of Frankenstein*, but it proved that John Elder, after creating a promising situation, was unable to exploit all the possibilities of the plot.

Bernard Robinson's designs were as good as ever and Hammer was certainly proving that it no longer mounted cheap productions. But although *Frankenstein Created Woman* was a workman-like and efficient horror film, it contained little of the Frankenstein myth.

Hammer was now mounting double-bills, and *Frankenstein Created Woman* went the rounds of the circuits in the company of *The Mummy's Shroud*, another routine mixture of murder and mayhem feebly linked to an Egyptian curse. Perhaps the company felt that Frankenstein needed the aid of a double-bill. Hammer's product did, however, manage to maintain, if not improve, its style and standards, and audiences showed no signs of tiring of the company's films, Hammer even being rewarded by the Queen's Award to Industry.

Two years later Peter Cushing reappeared as the Baron. This time Terence Fisher directed a film that returned to the standards achieved by the first two productions in the Hammer series when assistant director Bert Batt and producer Anthony Nelson-Keys put their heads together and concocted *Frankenstein Must be Destroyed*, a film that many regard as one of Britain's most accomplished horror films.

The film begins as a burglar, breaking into Frankenstein's laboratory, is shocked to discover a

lifeless body hanging up in a glass case. Suddenly he is attacked by a masked figure who turns out to be the Baron himself. Before the police can arrest him, Frankenstein flees to the town of Altenburg and takes refuge in the lodging house of Anna Spengler, whose fiancé, Dr Karl Holst, works at the local asylum. Frankenstein discovers that Karl has been stealing drugs to provide extra money for Anna and her mother, and the Baron blackmails the couple into helping his former colleague, Dr Brandt, an inmate at the asylum. Brandt had succeeded in transplanting a human brain and Frankenstein plans to bring him back to sanity and gain the secret of the operation. But no sooner is Brandt liberated than he dies of a heart attack.

Undaunted, Frankenstein decides to transplant Brandt's brain into the body of Professor Richter, the head of the asylum. But when Richter awakens after the operation, with Brandt's brain in his skull, he is horrified by his new appearance. He looks to Anna for help, but Anna imagines that he is threatening her and tries to stab him. Richter sets off to find his wife and Frankenstein kills Anna. The Baron starts to look for Richter and Karl follows, vowing vengeance on Frankenstein. Richter's wife is startled by her husband's appearance and runs from the house. Alone in the house, Richter sets a trap for

Hammer producer Anthony Nelson-Keys, who had a hand in many of the company's films and also helped to script *Frankenstein Must be Destroyed (Columbia–EMI–Warner)*

Frankenstein by luring him inside and starting a fire, and although Frankenstein rushes outside, Richter catches him and carries him back inside as the inferno rages. No one is spared in the final holocaust.

At last the series had achieved a successful change of formula. The production was uncompromising in its detail and achieved a nice sense of the gothic. Freddie Jones as Richter gave what is, without doubt, one of the finest performances in any Frankenstein film, achieving that rarest of all ingredients in a horror film, sensitivity.

Perhaps if the series had ended with this production it would have been a fitting climax. But there was still more money to be gained from the Baron's exploits, but by 1970 Hammer felt that it needed to ring the changes yet again in the Frankenstein saga. Hammer double-bills were now commonplace, offering cine-magoers *The Scars of Dracula* and *Horror of Frankenstein* in one show. The former was probably the worst of the Hammer Dracula films, while the latter was a sad and confused attempt to update the Frankenstein myth. This time, a younger Baron Frankenstein appeared in the shape of Ralph Bates, a highly effective actor, but no Peter Cushing. Jimmy

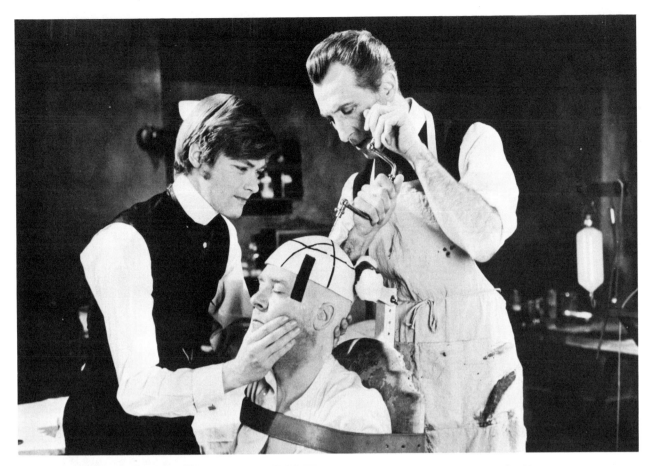

above : Simon Ward helps Peter Cushing to operate on Freddie Jones in *Frankenstein Must be Destroyed (Columbia–EMI–Warner)*

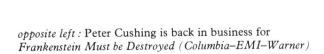

above : One of Hammer's finest leading ladies, Veronica Carlson, was a force to be reckoned with in *Frankenstein Must be Destroyed (Columbia–EMI–Warner)*

right : Grave-robber Dennis Price helps Victor Frankenstein (Ralph Bates) in *Horror of Frankenstein (Columbia–EMI–Warner)*

opposite left : Peter Cushing is back in business for *Frankenstein Must be Destroyed (Columbia–EMI–Warner)*

Ralph Bates and Graham James in *Horror of Frankenstein*
(*Columbia–EMI–Warner*)

Ralph Bates and Veronica Carlson are served a meal by
Kate O'Mara in *Horror of Frankenstein* (*Columbia–EMI–
Warner*)

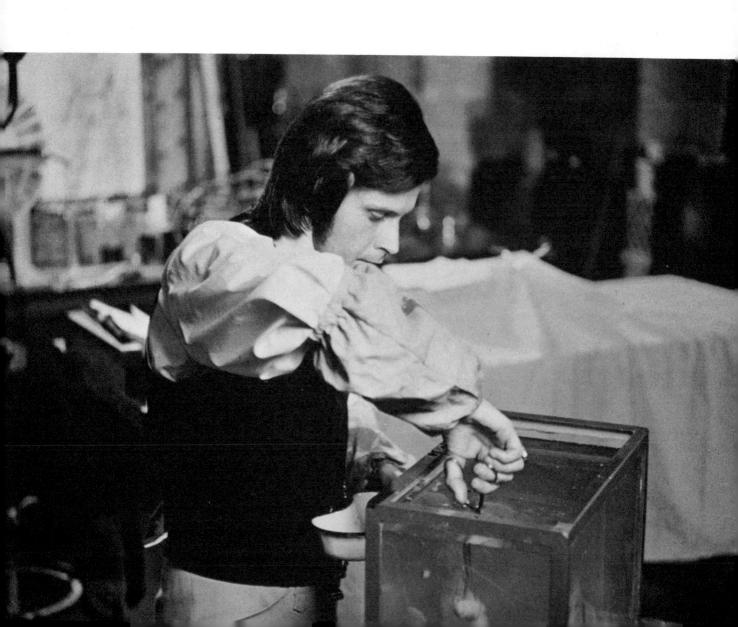

above : Dave Prowse as the Monster in *Horror of Frankenstein (Columbia–EMI–Warner)*

Baron Frankenstein (Ralph Bates) begins to piece together his latest Monster in *Horror of Frankenstein (Columbia–EMI–Warner)*

Sangster returned to the fold, not only writing the film, but directing it as well. It turned out to be a weak remake of *The Curse of Frankenstein* and was obviously aimed at a younger audience.

Baron Frankenstein was even more ruthless and aided by a husband and wife team of grave-robbers, played by Dennis Price and Joan Rice. Corpses littered the ground, sex abounded, black comedy was injected and the film contained what must be the most unintentionally comical monster ever to grace the screen. The sets were far from the standard achieved by Bernard Robinson and the entire production appeared sadly tatty.

The Monster, whose appearance would not have frightened a small child, was played by muscleman Dave Prowse, who was later to find fame as Darth Vader in the money-spinning *Star Wars*. Sangster went on to prove himself to be a highly effective director when he made another film for the company, the impressive *Lust for a Vampire*, but thankfully Hammer did not make a sequel to *Horror of Frankenstein*.

Three years later Hammer returned with another addition to its original series, and again saw fit to call upon the services of Peter Cushing. The script for *Frankenstein and the Monster from Hell* was from the pen of John Elder, and, once again, he proved that, although he could create an interesting situation, he had difficulty in expanding a plot.

Dr Simon Helder is imprisoned in a lunatic asylum at Carlsbad after being found guilty of grave-robbing. He later discovers that Baron Frankenstein is running the asylum and experimenting on the patients. Helder assists in Frankenstein's surgical operations, as the

Not knowing that Sarah (MADELINE SMITH) is mute, newcomer to the asylum Dr Helder (SHANE BRIANT) tries to talk to her as she bandages his wound. A scene from "FRANKENSTEIN and the MONSTER FROM HELL".

JOSEPH E. LEVINE PRESENTS AN AVCO EMBASSY PICTURE
A HAMMER FILM PRODUCTION

FRANKENSTEIN
AND THE
MONSTER FROM HELL;
Starring   PETER CUSHING · SHANE BRIANT
MADELINE SMITH

SCREENPLAY BY JOHN ELDER PRODUCED BY ROY SKEGGS DIRECTED BY TERENCE FISHER
AN AVCO EMBASSY RELEASE

Dr Helder (Shane Briant) tries to talk to Sarah (Madeline Smith), not knowing that she is mute, in *Frankenstein and the Monster from Hell* (*Avco–Embassy*)

Baron is still unable to use his hands for the intricate manoeuvres involved. Frankenstein pieces together one of the inmates after an accident and saves his life, but in the process turns him into a Monster, and when the Baron transfers another brain into his new creation, the Monster goes wild. In the grand finale the creature is torn limb from limb by the other inmates after Frankenstein has attempted to mate him with a female prisoner.

Terence Fisher made a welcome return to the series and created some memorable images, but the script still undermined the many possibilities in the plot. It seemed that the company was turning even further away from Mary Shelley. Dave Prowse made his second appearance as the Monster, this time with totally different make-up, which made him look like a cross between an ape and a man. The film also took nearly a year to achieve a release in Britain, where it was double-billed with a cheap Kung Fu epic. Perhaps the public was growing tired of the Baron and his creation.

Hammer produced three highly effective Frankenstein films. The rest are, at best, nothing more than standard programmes. At present there is no sign of another Frankenstein film for the company, and it seems that another chapter of the Frankenstein saga may have drawn to a close.

Peter Cushing in his final appearance to date as the Baron in *Frankenstein and the Monster from Hell* (*Avco–Embassy*)

The Bodysnatcher (PATRICK TROUGHTON) is disturbed by the arrival of a Police Sergeant as he is about to lift the corpse out of the grave. A scene from the film "FRANKENSTEIN and the MONSTER FROM HELL".

A body-snatcher (Patrick Troughton) about to lift a corpse from its grave in *Frankenstein and the Monster from Hell* (*Avco–Embassy*)
Peter Cushing and Shane Briant as his new assistant in *Frankenstein and the Monster from Hell* (*Avco–Embassy*)

6 Teenage Monsters Unite

While the British Frankenstein revival was taking place, America had also realized that there were still a few dollars to be made from the old Monster. But the once glorious name of Frankenstein was about to be besmirched.

American International Studios were producing low-budget horror films, when a young producer called Herman Cohen hit the financial nail on the head. The film that began his run of good luck was *I was a Teenage Werewolf*, a weak reworking of the old lycanthrope legend set in a high school, starring Michael Landon before he became better known to television viewers as Little Joe in *Bonanza*. American International had its biggest financial success and demanded that Cohen return to the teenage monster market. So in 1957 Cohen and director Herbert L. Strock turned their attention to Frankenstein.

I was a Teenage Frankenstein was a conventional fifties horror film. A descendant of Frankenstein, played by Whit Bissel, continues to practice his ancestor's experiments in modern-day America. He is ruthless, equipped with a laboratory that the lowliest chemistry student would have scorned and possesses some astonishing luck. Car accidents keep happening on his doorstep and provide him with a convenient spare-parts service.

One such crash is the source of most of the body for his Monster, but, alas, the face of the animated being leaves much to be desired, and the Monster leaves the laboratory for a rampage with the local co-eds, during which he kills a young man. The doctor grafts the corpse's head onto the creature, but when Frankenstein plans to dismantle the creature to export it to Europe, the Monster reacts in a predictable way: Frankenstein is killed and his creation electrocuted.

It was not the most original of plots, but it did have one or two hilarious lines. On discovering that the Monster can cry, Frankenstein yells "Look the tear ducts work". And later he taunts the monster with: "You have a tongue in your head. I know, I put it there."

The film was a smash hit and out-grossed its predecessor. It also contained a rather pointless innovation for a Frankenstein film: in the closing scenes the screen burst into colour. Perhaps the budget didn't allow for a full-colour production.

The Monster in *I was a Teenage Frankenstein* together with the Teenage Werewolf returned the following year in an enjoyable little film, *How to Make a Monster*. A Hollywood make-up artist discovers that he is about to be made redundant because his studio has decided to stop producing horror films.

He gains control of two young actors, whom he sends out to terrorize the neighbourhood, disguised as film monsters. Inevitably, the make-up man ends up in a fiery finale. Once again Herbert L. Strock directed the film and produced his most enjoyable fantasy.

But American International didn't have it all its own way; other companies were turning their attention to Frankenstein. Allied Artists had the brainwave of looking to the future and coaxed Boris Karloff into starring in *Frankenstein 1970*. This time another member of the Frankenstein family, Karloff, is discovered at work on unholy experiments, and it's not long before he journeys to the castle vault to unearth the family Monster and revive him with the help of an atomic reactor. However, matters are complicated by a television company, which is making a film at the old family home. As usual, the experiments go wrong and the Baron and his Monster are killed by a leak from the reactor, the final revelation showing that the Monster's face had been modelled on his creator. The only remotely chilling sequence in the film occurred at the beginning, when a monster chases a girl through a wood, a scene enhanced by some highly effective camera work. But, surprise, surprise, it's only a film company making its latest horror production.

The film also proved that Cinemascope was not the ideal process for a horror film. Karloff was also dissatisfied with *Frankenstein 1970* and said that no one knew how to make a decent terror film any longer.

If Karloff was depressed by his latest film, he should have been thankful that he did not have to appear in *Frankenstein's Daughter*, a poverty-row effort made in the same year. The sets were cheap, the cast uninspired, the script deplorable, and the direction non-existent. This time yet another descendant of the Frankenstein family has found his way to America. The title is somewhat misleading, since Frankenstein's daughter never appeared in the film: the title was derived from a nick-name given to the Monster by Frankenstein who had constructed his latest creation mostly from the body of a girl, although the finished product was in no way feminine. The only mildly startling moment in this shabby production was when a young man in a monster mask leapt from behind a bush at a girl. Perhaps they should have invited him to play the Monster. Unfortunately *Frankenstein's Daughter* was not alone in its awfulness as the following years were to prove.

However, 1958 did provide cinemagoers with one intelligent variation on the Frankenstein theme: Eugene Lourie, a director with much experience of

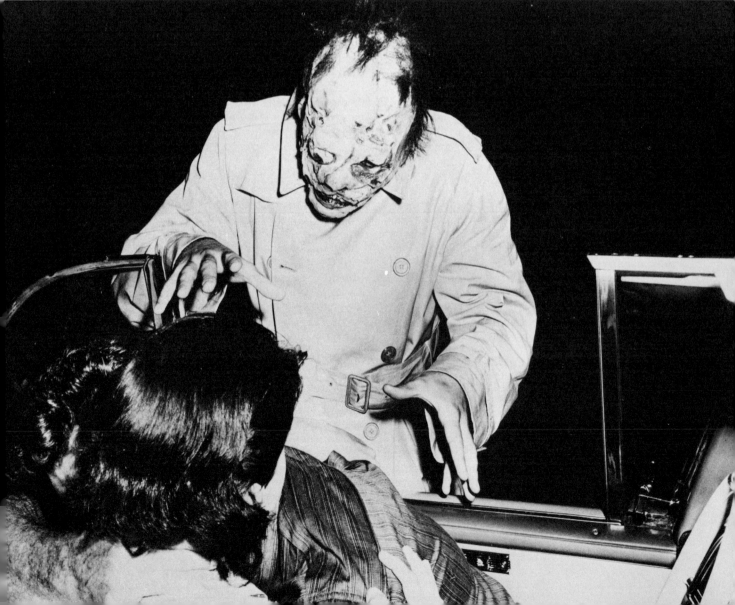

left : Michael Landon tries to come to terms with a problem that doesn't confront many teenagers – how to stop changing into a savage wolf-like creature. *I was a Teenage Werewolf* was producer Herman Cohen's first attempt to create monsters for the teenage market *(American International)*

opposite below : Gary Conway menaces a couple in *I was a Teenage Frankenstein (American International)*

right : Gary Conway threatens the world in *I was a Teenage Frankenstein (American International)*

below : Gary Conway as the youngest Frankenstein Monster menaces yet another girl. The advertising of *I was a Teenage Frankenstein* leaves little to the imagination *(American International)*

BODY OF A BOY...
MIND OF A MONSTER..
SOUL OF AN
UNEARTHLY THING!

"TEENAGE FRANKENSTEIN" CERT.

Starring: WHIT BISSELL · PHYLLIS COATES · ROBERT BURTON · GARY CONWAY.

ANGLO AMALGAMATED FILM DISTRIBUTORS LTD.

ADULTS ONLY

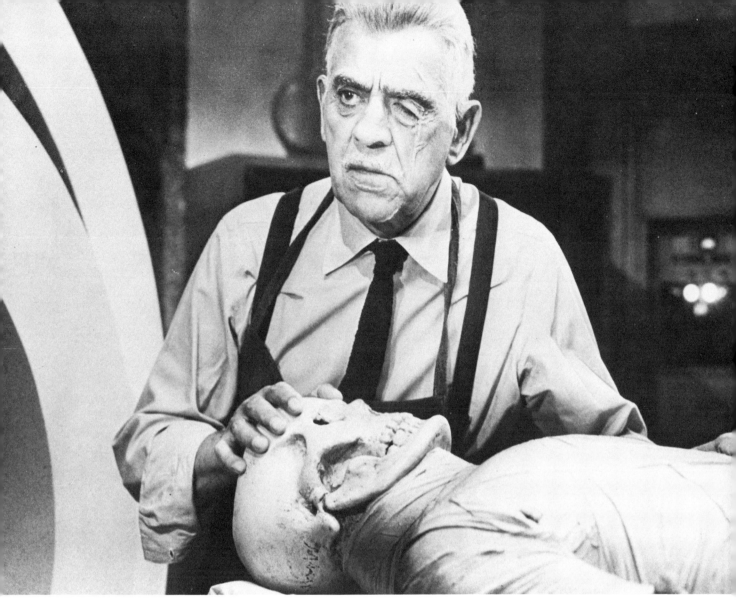

above : Boris Karloff contemplates his latest creation in
Frankenstein 1970 (Allied Artists)

right : Boris Karloff in *Frankenstein 1970 (Allied Artists)*

opposite left : A teenage werewolf unites with a teenage
Frankenstein Monster to demonstrate *How to Make a
Monster (American International)*

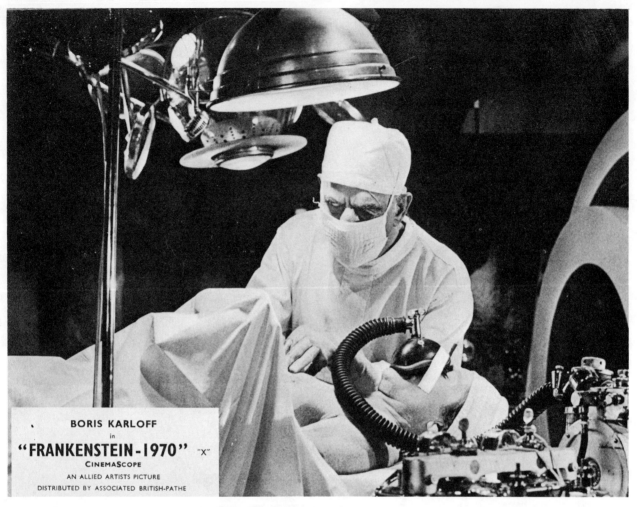

BORIS KARLOFF
in
"FRANKENSTEIN-1970" "X"
CinemaScope
AN ALLIED ARTISTS PICTURE
DISTRIBUTED BY ASSOCIATED BRITISH-PATHE

Boris Karloff in *Frankenstein 1970* (*Allied Artists*)

special effects, was responsible for *The Colossus of New York*, the story of a scientist whose son is the victim of a car accident. The son's brain is transferred into the body of a giant robot but does not appreciate its new home and destroys the robot. At long last the pathos necessary to the Frankenstein story returned. Lourie even used a child to demonstrate that it took innocence to understand the feelings of a brain trapped within the hell of a mechanical body.

America produced its next Frankenstein film in 1962, but *House on Bare Mountain* was far from what cinemagoers had come to expect from Hollywood horror. The permissive sixties had arrived and the Monster was merely one of the strange creatures that arrived for a nude party in an old house. The Monster and Count Dracula were revealed to be ordinary partygoers in fancy dress.

Another cinematic oddity also appeared in 1962, when director Roger Kay brought out a thriller entitled *The Cabinet of Dr Caligari*. The film bore hardly any resemblance to Robert Wiene's original, and could not be classified as a remake. Glynis Johns plays a tourist travelling through Europe who is trapped in a mysterious house with a group of people suffering from various mental disorders. Lurking in the shadows is the mysterious figure of Dr Caligari, whose identity the audience is invited to guess. Lost

opposite above : Trudy Morton is the victim of one of Oliver Frankenstein's experiments and turns into a hideous creature in *Frankenstein's Daughter* (*Astor*)

right : Oliver Frankenstein (Donald Murphy) prepares to complete his latest experiment in *Frankenstein's Daughter* (*Astor*)

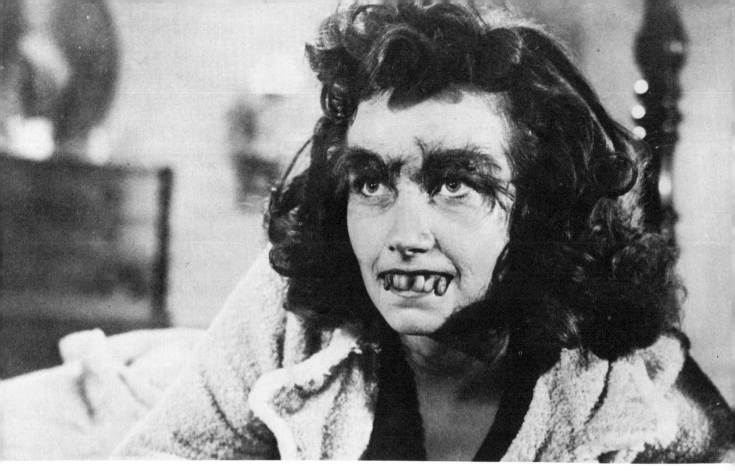

FRANKENSTEIN'S DAUGHTER

starring
JOHN ASHLEY
SANDRA KNIGHT

A new, but vastly inferior, version of *The Cabinet of Dr Caligari* (20th Century-Fox)

in this sorry mess are such fine actors as Dan O'Herlihy and Lawrence Dobkin, who, like Miss Johns, make valiant attempts to save the film. But the production is sunk, surprisingly enough, by Robert Bloch's screenplay, although Roger Kay's direction is never inspired, and proves that Cinemascope is not the ideal medium for a thriller. The reason for the film's production remains its greatest mystery.

In the same year Vincent Price starred in *Twice Told Tales*, three stories from the pen of Nathaniel Hawthorne. The first one, *Dr Heidegger's Experiment*, starred Sebastian Cabot as the doctor of the title who discovers an elixir of youth and uses it to rejuvenate both himself and his friend Alex Medbourne (Vincent Price). Together they use the drug to bring back to life Heidegger's bride, Sylvia. But when Heidegger learns that Alex was responsible for her death, a fight ensues in which Heidegger is killed, and Alex watches as the newly revived Sylvia returns to dust and bone. Sidney Salkow directed with little flair, and any enjoyment there is comes from the performances of Price and Cabot.

In 1964 the Athletic Models' Guild was responsible for the first homosexual Frankenstein film, *Angelic Frankenstein*. Bob Mizer was credited as the director while the rest of the cast and crew hid behind a blanket of anonymity.

The following year Barry Mahon directed another epic for the soft-porn market called *Fanny Hill meets*

Ed Wolff played the giant robot with the brain of a man in *The Colossus of New York* (Paramount)

Dr Erotico. This was, in fact, a sequel to the earlier *Fanny Hill meets Lady Chatterley* and an undistinguished continuation of Miss Hill's adventures.

Fanny Hill pays another visit to Lady Chatterley, but discovers that the family home has been taken over by Dr Erotico, a scientist whose experiments are similar to those of Frankenstein. There is even a Monster in the laboratory waiting to be activated, and it is not long before Fanny Hill has accidentally re-activated the creature. But the Monster falls in love with Fanny with disastrous results, and meets a fiery death.

In 1965 Frankenstein visited the Wild West when Circle Productions decided to make two films in which two of the toughest outlaws tangled with two of Europe's most popular monsters. *Billy the Kid versus Dracula* was made back-to-back with *Jesse James meets Frankenstein's Daughter*. Both films were made by the same crew and on the slimmest of budgets. Veteran director William Beaudine was chosen to mastermind both productions, but neither western nor horror fans could find much to enthuse about in either film, particularly *Jesse James meets Frankenstein's Daughter*.

Rudolph and Maria Frankenstein, the Baron's grandchildren, flee to Mexico where they plan to continue their experiments. Their grandfather had created a small number of artificial brains and Rudolph and Maria try in vain to transplant them successfully. They now have only one brain left, and

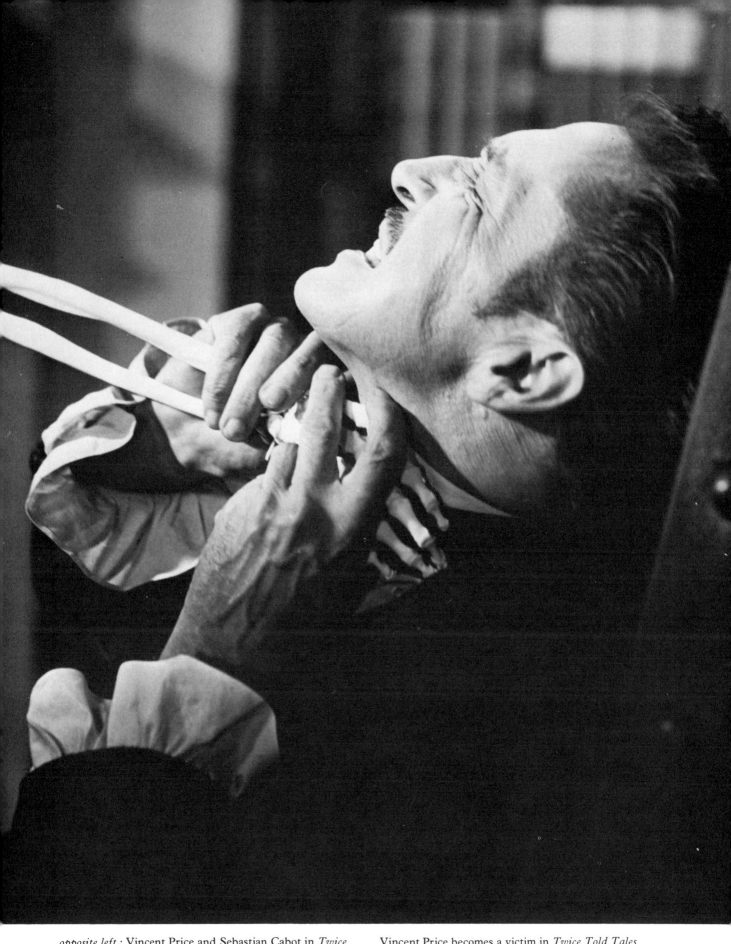

opposite left : Vincent Price and Sebastian Cabot in *Twice Told Tales (Admiral/Tigon)*

Vincent Price becomes a victim in *Twice Told Tales (Admiral/Tigon)*

A posse on the trail of a monster in *Jesse James Meets Frankenstein's Daughter* (Avco–Embassy)

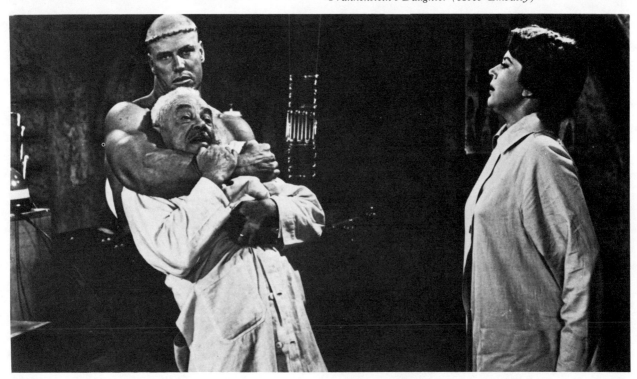

Maria Frankenstein has a disagreement with her brother while the Monster puts the squeeze on him in *Jesse James Meets Frankenstein's Daughter* (Avco–Embassy)

the next operation just has to work.

Enter roving outlaw Jesse James and his muscle-bound friend Hank. Maria decides that Hank's body is the ideal home for a new brain and operates on the wounded outlaw, turning him into a new Frankenstein Monster. But, as usual, the old Frankenstein luck runs out and Maria is throttled by her creation.

The film did not betray much invention and its low budget meant that the production was sadly tatty. It seemed that the art director could not live up to many of the lines in the script. "Let's go into the library", Maria urges Jesse James; and they enter a

above : Is Maria Frankenstein using a crash helmet to revive her Monster? It certainly looks like one *(Avco-Embassy)*

Jesse James in the arms of the Monster *(Avco–Embassy)*

room that contains no books at all. The laboratory is a lack-lustre affair and there is a bottle that is actually labelled "Poison", not to mention some thought-transference equipment that looks suspiciously like modified motor cycle crash-helmets. However there was one saving grace: a barn-storming performance by Narda Onyx as Maria Frankenstein. The Monster never went west again.

But if the great American outdoors proved unfriendly to Mary Shelley's creation, outer space proved downright hostile. *Frankenstein meets the Space Monster* was made in 1965 and used its catchpenny title to draw its audience into watching a mediocre space opera containing some of the worst special effects to come out of Hollywood. The story concerned a robot astronaut whose face and circuits suffer severe damage when it tackles an alien threat from outer space.

The script was at pains to make excuses for the use of the title and people constantly referred to the robot as a "Frankenstein". In Britain the film was released under the more honest but less potentially appealing title, *Duel of the Space Monsters*. Usually in this kind of undistinguished production some enjoyment can be derived from the sheer awfulness of the film, but *Frankenstein meets the Space Monster* proved to be an exception to the rule: it bored its audience.

Meanwhile across the border in 1969, the Canadian Film Development Corporation helped to finance a modest effort called *Flick*, known in other parts of the world as *Frankenstein on Campus*. Another member of the Frankenstein family finds his way to Canada and enrols at a University. It's not long before he's carrying out more experiments, this time to control the minds of his fellow students. A neat twist in an otherwise uninteresting production has Frankenstein falling to his death, only to be revealed as a robot. A professor at the university has been responsible for his construction. Somehow the Frankenstein myth fitted uneasily into a campus setting at a time when student unrest was a more compelling problem. *Flick* did not spawn a sequel and it is easy to see why. Updating the Frankenstein story was indeed a difficult task.

In the same year Universal released a film that was obviously inspired by Mary Shelley. *The Forbin Project* replaced the conventional Monster with a computer called Colossus, which is responsible for the West's nuclear defences, while the Russians have a computer, Guardian, which performs a similar function. When both sides decide to unite machines,

A robot astronaut is in need of repair when *Frankenstein Meets the Space Monster*

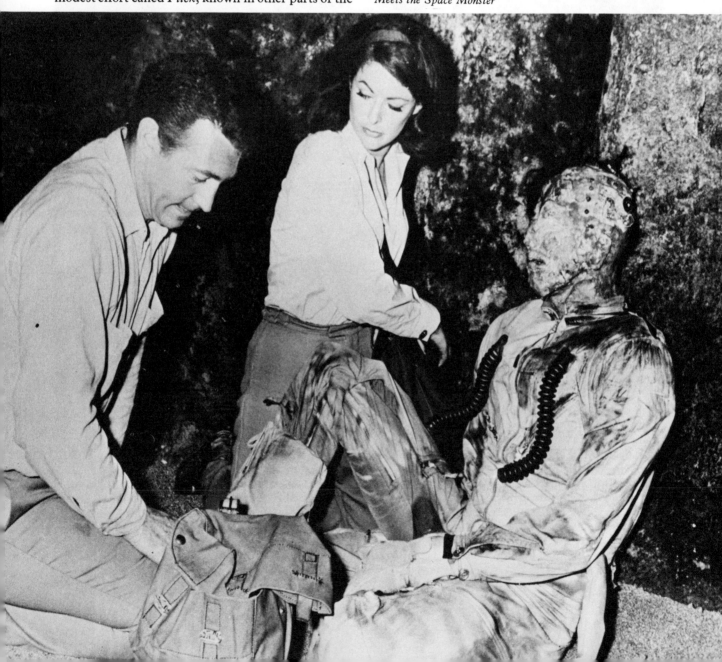

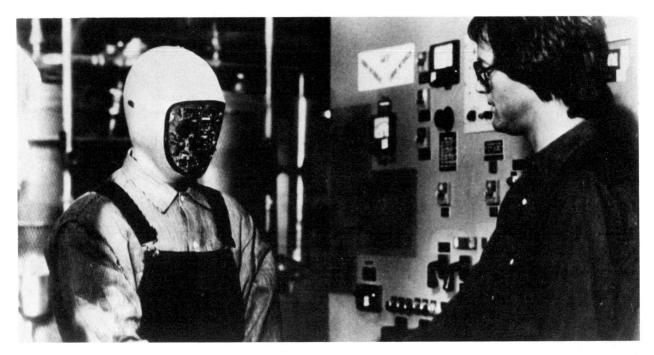

trouble follows. Charles Forbin, the creator of the computer, attempts to sabotage its schemes to dominate the world, but Colossus foils his plans. In the end Forbin faces defeat when Colossus tells him that in the fullness of time he will grow to love his creation.

The Forbin Project was a brave attempt to tackle one of the main Frankenstein themes in an unusual and intelligent manner. In Britain it was not released until 1972 and its running time was reduced by some 12 minutes. Joseph Sargent handled his production with much expertise, and it is a pity that the distributors could not market the film in a more positive way.

In 1971 another attempt was made to wring a few more dollars from the Monster. Independent International Pictures recruited Lon Chaney Jr and J. Carrol Naish for a horror film called *The Blood Seekers*, but the production ran into problems and the company was in danger of ending up with no film at all, partly because the film drastically underran and partly because there were a number of continuity lapses. But help was at hand: the script was totally re-written with an eye to the box office and ended up as *Dracula versus Frankenstein*, with a plot story-line distilled from plots already tried in previous films.

Count Dracula revives the Frankenstein Monster with the help of the last surviving member of the Frankenstein family. But the Monster's revival leads to a trail of death and destruction: Frankenstein meets his death on a guillotine, and the Monster and Count Dracula are left to battle it out. Surprisingly the Count wins by tearing the Monster to pieces, but, as (ill) luck would have it, the rays of the morning sun appear and the vampire crumbles to dust.

J. Carrol Naish played Frankenstein and attempted to inject some life into the proceedings, while Lon Chaney Jr played a homicidal brute called Groton but was given little opportunity to shine. The worst

Chuck (Peter Fonda) meets an old but friendly robot called Clarke when he visits *Futureworld (American International/Brent Walker)*

performance, however, came from Zandor Vorkov, who, as Count Dracula, added a ludicrous element to the film. The production also featured one of the shabbiest Monsters ever in the person of John Bloom, whose only distinguishing feature was his height of seven feet four inches. The editor of *Famous Monsters of Filmland* magazine, Forrest J. Ackerman, also appeared in this sorry mess and it is to be hoped that he shed a tear for what was happening to the Frankenstein saga.

In 1973 science-fiction writer Michael Crichton turned director for MGM's *Westworld*, the story of a playground of the future where fantasies can be indulged thanks to an army of programmed robots. One of these pleasure centres is called "Westworld" and represents the frontier days of the old west. Yul Brynner, dressed as he was in *The Magnificent Seven*, plays a robot gunfighter who is constantly challenging visitors to a shoot-out and is programmed to lose. But the robots revolt and "Westworld" becomes a nightmare.

This ingenious variation on the Frankenstein theme was extremely successful, and in 1976 a sequel appeared called *Futureworld*, in which Peter Fonda starred as a reporter investigating the re-opening of the ill-fated pleasure centre. But a sinister plot has been hatched to kidnap world statesmen and replace them with robot duplicates. Even Peter Fonda finds himself facing a mechanical double who threatens to kill him. Richard Heffron skilfully directed the sequel, which was made, surprisingly enough, by American International.

By 1974 the Frankenstein series had again moved with the times. Black actors were making inroads into the film industry and as black heroes were now

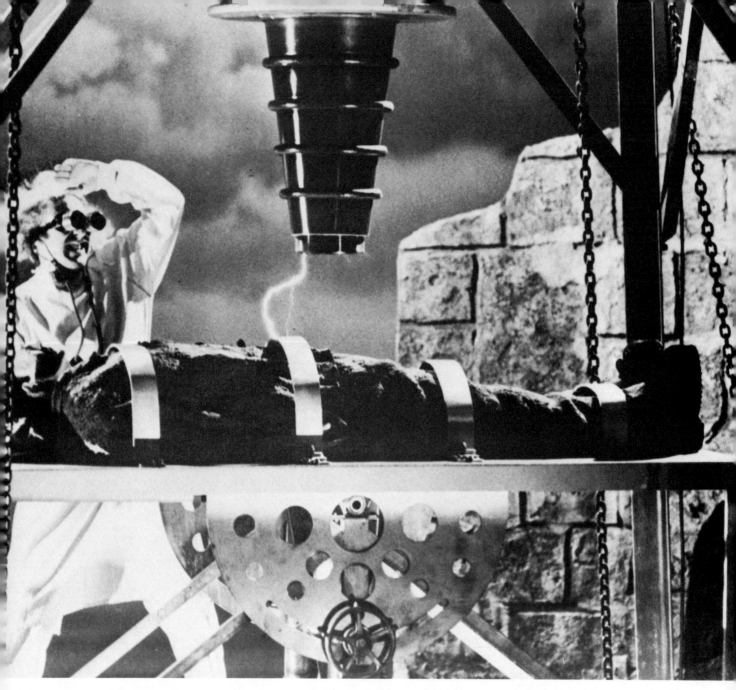

commonplace, how about black villains? American International had produced a successful black version of the Dracula legend, *Blacula*, although much of its success had been generated by that fine actor William Marshal, and the company turned its attention to Frankenstein and produced *Blackenstein*, the story of a black GI whose body is torn apart in Vietnam and pieced together later. Somehow the plot was too tied to the realities of the Vietnam War for comfort and the film did not spawn a sequel, whereas *Scream, Blacula Scream* repeated a successful formula.

The following year, however, produced one of the most successful Frankenstein films of recent years. Horror films certainly lend themselves to satire, but more often than not the jokes are crude and simple. In *Young Frankenstein*, however, the jokes were carefully calculated and became a tribute to the genre and the fine craftsmen of the thirties.

Gene Wilder brings Peter Boyle to life in *Young Frankenstein (20th Century-Fox)*

Writer and director Mel Brooks has an erratic talent: at his best hilarious, at his worst he is undisciplined and self-indulgent. *Blazing Saddles* demonstrates a talent that sometimes fails to realize when a joke is fully played out. However with *Young Frankenstein* Mel Brooks was in full control, displaying not only a great knowledge of the Frankenstein saga, but a great love for it as well. He also chose to film in black and white so that he could achieve a photographic similarity to the Universal series. The sets were beautifully constructed to evoke the thirties flavour and the make-up was magnificently stylized.

Gene Wilder plays a descendant of the Frankenstein family who lectures in surgery in America. He is very conscious of the notoriety attached to his name and insists on being addressed as "Fronkenstein". But it's not long before he inherits the family estate in Transylvania and travels to the old castle, on a train that is a magnificent copy of the one used in *Son of Frankenstein*.

Frankenstein is met at the station by the faithful Igor, played by Marty Feldman, a hunchback whose hump has a habit of moving from shoulder to shoulder. Like all the family fanatics before him, Frankenstein cannot resist reviving the Monster, a role accomplished with great skill by Peter Boyle. Frankenstein brings modern science to bear on the project and instead of clamps on the head the Monster now possesses a zip fastener.

With such a wealth of detail it is difficult to single out high spots in a film in which there are so many fine moments. Gene Hackman's hilarious appearance as the blind hermit, obviously modelled on O. P. Heggie's performance in *The Bride of Frankenstein*, is a *tour de force*, as he attempts to help the Monster to food and drink but succeeds only in inflicting accidental pain. Gene Wilder has many magnificent moments as Frankenstein and successfully apes Colin Clive's cry of "It's alive, it's alive!"

One of the funniest scenes finds the Monster meeting a small girl who invites him to play with her on a see-saw, but the Monster's weight catapults her into the air, through a window, and into her bed. The joke is based on the sequence in the 1931 film in which Karloff's Monster meets a small child on the river bank.

Young Frankenstein is perhaps the most successful and pleasing satire on the horror genre, and Wilder and Brooks created a film that was a loving tribute to the Universal Frankenstein saga.

Little of true worth had come from the American Frankenstein films of the fifties, sixties, and seventies. The majority were trash, although probably profitable, but films like *Young Frankenstein* proved that the theme could still be treated with imagination and success. It showed that someone somewhere still cared about standards.

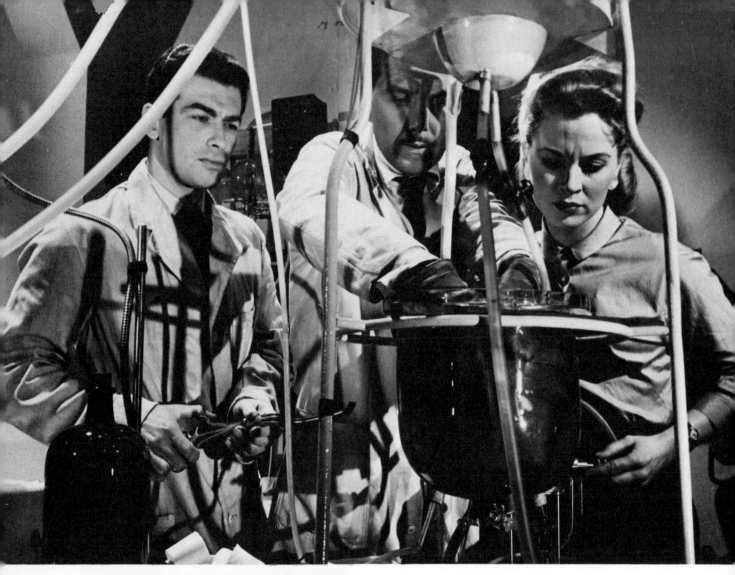

Robert Hutton (centre) is the scientist responsible for reviving a dormant brain in *Man without a Body (Eros)*

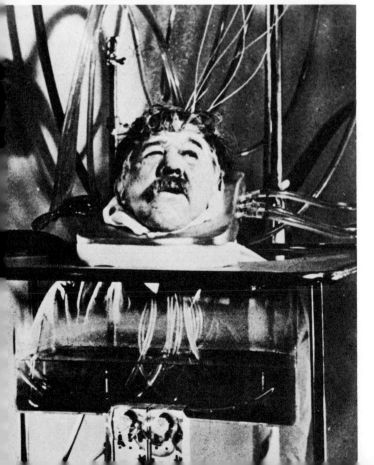

The Head – another variation on the Frankenstein theme (*Trans-Lux*)

7 More British and even some Continental Blood

Just as Hammer was about to embark on its Frankenstein cycle, another British company, Eros, was launching itself into the low-budget horror field. In 1957 the company was responsible for a variation on the Frankenstein theme called *Man without a Body*. W. Lee Wilder, the brother of Billy Wilder, was brought to Britain to share directorial credit with Charles Saunders, but the result was a lack-lustre production, telling the story of a wealthy businessman who finances the experiments of a scientist, played by Robert Hutton. They plan to revive the head of Nostradamus in the hope that it will run a business empire, but Nostradamus is none too keen on the idea, and when his head is grafted on to a new body he becomes yet another cinematic monster.

The film had many unintentionally funny moments but failed to produce even a mild shock. The only surprise was to find that fine actor George Coulouris taking part in such a worthless piece. Frankenstein had his rivals but they were not proving very successful.

Another head-grafting experiment took place in Germany in 1959, when Victor Trivas wrote and directed *Die Nackte und der Satan*, which was released in Britain and the United States as *The Head*. It also marked a return to the screen of art director Hermann Warm, who had designed the sets for the 1919 version of *The Cabinet of Dr Caligari*.

Professor Abel has kept alive the severed head of a dog by the use of Serum Z. But Abel is suffering from a fatal heart condition, and when Dr Ood offers to perform a transplant operation Abel agrees. Instead of giving him a new heart, however, however, Ood severs Abel's head and connects it to a life-support machine. When Abel realizes what has happened he is horrified and refuses to divulge the secret of his serum, which, it appears, has the power to prolong life. Ood, like all good mad scientists, continues his operations and grafts the head of Abel's assistant, Irene, on to the body of a stripper. But the police have at last tumbled to Ood's plans and, as he attempts to escape, he suffers a dizzy spell and falls to a well-deserved death. Dr Abel's head is finally allowed to rest in peace.

Die Nackte und der Satan has little to commend it apart from Michel Simon's performance as Dr Abel, which, in the English-language version, is ruined by some awful dubbing. But Horst Frank, as Dr Ood, is a stereotyped mad scientist, and the rest of the cast are undistinguished. The film also has one of the worst musical scores ever heard in the cinema.

By 1960 Hammer's success in the horror market had sparked off many imitations. *Doctor Blood's Coffin*, directed by Sidney J. Furie, was yet another variation on the Frankenstein theme. Dr Peter Blood returns from Vienna to a small village in Cornwall, firm in the knowledge that he has now the power to transplant human hearts, and soon some of the local villagers are discovered with their hearts ripped out. The final test of Blood's experiments is to revive a corpse by the use of a new heart. As a nurse has spurned the doctor's advances, Blood decides to bring her dead husband back to life. But there are the usual disastrous results, for the newly revived corpse promptly carries the doctor off to his death in a disused mine.

The production was as gory as anything Hammer had achieved, but lacked a certain style and suffered from a weak script. On the credit side there were some good Cornish locations and some crisp photography.

Hammer's films had become very popular on the Continent of Europe, with Terence Fisher being accorded cult status in France and the company's films receiving excellent critical reviews. It was no wonder that other countries attempted to emulate Hammer's success.

In 1964 Spain launched its first Frankenstein film, *El Testamento del Frankenstein*, which was directed by Jose Luis Madrid and starred Gerard Landry and George Vallis. But several years elapsed before the Spaniards returned to the myth. Spanish cinemagoers seemed to prefer their horror to be less scientific, and many Spanish horror films deal with vampires and werewolves.

The "Carry On" series of comedies turned its attention to horror films in 1966 and came up with *Carry on Screaming*. Inspector Bung (Harry H. Corbett), investigates a number of strange happenings taking place around the home of Dr Watt (Kenneth Williams). The scientist has created a monster called Odd Bodd, who has a habit of going for midnight strolls and alarming the locals. Odd Bodd's severed finger grows into another creature called Odd Bodd Junior. Not content with concocting these monsters, Watt also revives an Egyptian mummy.

You either like the "Carry On" films or you don't. If you are looking for satire and wit, then *Carry on Screaming* is not for you. It is a run-of-the-mill British comedy with an excellent cast, including such series regulars as Joan Sims, Charles Hawtrey, and Jim Dale. The film is filled to the brim with Talbot Rothwell's usual puns and the laughs are there—but the jokes are old. Perhaps screenwriter Rothwell relied too heavily on his cast.

In the same year Herbert J. Leger wrote, produced,

and directed *It*, a new version of the Golem legend. Not since the 1936 Czechoslovakian–French version, *Le Golem*, had anyone attempted to revitalize the man of stone. Roddy McDowall was brought to Britain to head the cast as Arthur Pimm, an assistant museum curator who discovers how to bring life to the giant stone statue. Pimm uses the statue to revenge himself on those who have incurred his displeasure and is delighted to discover that the Golem is indestructible. Hammersmith Bridge is brought down by the statue, which, with Pimm, takes refuge in a large country house. But the police are hot on the trail and a nuclear device finally destroys the building. Pimm is dead, but the Golem is unharmed, and walks off into the sea.

Many of the ideas in the film were quite promising, but it seems that not enough cash was on hand to realize most of them. The Golem itself looks more like a perambulating tree and could not compete with any of its predecessors. Pimm's mother is in reality a rotting corpse that he still worships, a direct crib from Hitchcock's *Psycho*, but quite effective for all that.

Kieron Moore (right) as Dr Peter Blood in *Doctor Blood's Coffin (Caralan/United Artists)*

But the destruction of Hammersmith Bridge is decidedly tatty and lets the film down. Roddy McDowall, a dapper hand at playing neurotic villains, copes well with the role of Pimm and receives good support from the rest of the cast. The Golem has yet to make another appearance.

Back in Spain in 1968 Enrique L. Equiliz directed *La Marca del Hombre Lobo*, starring one of Europe's most popular horror actors, Paul Naschy. It was the story of a man who killed a werewolf but was bitten by the creature and tainted with its curse. He also fell under the influence of a vampire. As you can see, the story has nothing to do with the Frankenstein myth nor any of its associated themes. So why does it warrant a mention here? The reason is that an American distributor bought up the film and decided to market it in a rather underhand fashion by changing the title to *Frankenstein's Bloody Terror* and even

putting a monster resembling the traditional image of the creature on the posters. The excuse for the title was to be found in a piece of narrative that was tacked on to the opening of the American prints, informing the audience that the Frankenstein family had changed its name to Wolfstein after being tainted with the curse of the werewolf. Audiences must have felt cheated by this deception. In Britain the film was screened as *Hell's Creatures*.

Paul Naschy was seen two years later in a more genuine entry to the Frankenstein series, *El Hombre que Vino Ummo*, which was released in English-speaking countries as *Dracula versus Frankenstein*. Science fiction mingled with more conventional horror in this film directed by Tulio Demichelli. The plot itself reads like a farce and almost turned out that way.

Michael Rennie is the leader of a group of invading aliens who take over the bodies of earth scientists. They plan to revive the planet's most dreaded creatures—Dracula, the Wolfman, the Mummy, and

Joan Sims becomes a living statue with the help of Dr Watt (Kenneth Williams), his sister (Fenella Fielding), and two monsters in *Carry on Screaming (EMI)*

the Frankenstein Monster—but things go wrong for the visitors from outer space when they begin to experience the human emotions of their new bodies. The Wolfman rebels against the alien plan and turns on the other monsters. The inevitable fiery climax ensues and the aliens are beaten.

Considering that the film was co-produced by three companies and originally filmed in 70 mm, what finally appeared on the screen seemed to suffer from a skimped budget. Dracula and the Frankenstein Monster never had the confrontation promised in the title and it was sad to see Michael Rennie lending his talents to such worthless rubbish. All in all, *Dracula versus Frankenstein* betrayed all the worst elements of the Spanish horror film, including a nasty line in torture. Paul Naschy was again seen as a werewolf, but his appearance counted for little.

Roddy McDowall comforts his mother in *It (Goldstar)*

The following year, 1971, saw another Spanish version of the Frankenstein saga, this time the work of one of Spain's most prolific directors, Jesus Franco. A one-time assistant to Orson Welles, Franco has carved a niche for himself in the low-budget horror genre. In 1961 he had made *The Horrible Dr Orloff (The Demon Doctor)*, the story of a ruthless scientist whose experiments were along the lines that Frankenstein had been pioneering. Although obviously made on a low budget, its atmospheric black-and-white photography lent it a certain style.

By 1971 Franco had decided to combine the Frankenstein legend with the Dracula saga. The result was *Dracula contra el Dr Frankenstein*, which featured an aging Dennis Price as Frankenstein and the French actor, Howard Vernon, as Count Dracula. Franco made no secret of the fact that he worked quickly, and the resulting film has more than a few rough edges.

The plot concerns the creation of a Frankenstein Monster, who, it is hoped, will put an end to Count Dracula's murderous activities. Meanwhile another doctor sets out to cure the vampire of his blood disorder. The Monster was played by Fernando Bilbao, an imposing actor, seven feet tall, whose appearance was quite impressive. However the film itself was dull and lifeless, although it was successful enough to spawn a sequel, *La Hija de Dracula*, in which Howard Vernon returned to the role of Dracula. This time there was no sign of Frankenstein or his Monster.

Another distinguished actor was enlisted to play Baron Frankenstein when Joseph Cotten starred in *La Figlia di Frankenstein (Lady Frankenstein)*. This 1971 Italian production was directed by Ernst Von Theumer, who chose to hide behind the name of Mel E. Welles. He made a sensible decision.

Tania Frankenstein, the daughter of the great man, returns to the family castle a fully qualified surgeon. Her father and his colleague, Dr Charles Williams, have been experimenting with the re-animation of corpses and finally succeed in bringing one of their creations to life, but unfortunately the Monster kills the Baron and goes off on the rampage. Tania convinces Dr Williams that the only way to defeat the Monster is to create another. Williams, who is madly in love with Tania, agrees to let her transplant his brain into the body of a muscular stable-boy. The original Monster reappears and Williams, in his new body, defeats it. In a scene that must be unique to the Frankenstein series, the scientist and Monster make love. But joy is short lived as Williams throttles Tania.

The posters for *Lady Frankenstein* give an accurate representation of the film: "Only the Monster she made could satisfy her strange desires", it proclaimed.

86

The Golem walks again, this time in the British-made *It*
(*Goldstar*)

The production was sadly undistinguished. The cast
included Mickey Hargitay as a musclebound policeman who appeared to have strayed in from another
film, and only Joseph Cotten offered anything remotely
resembling a good performance. David Pirie in the
British Film Institute's Monthly Film Bulletin found
the film a thoroughly nasty experience:

> The emphasis throughout is on crude physical detail (the
> Hammer Frankensteins are models of restraint by
> comparison), and the Monster struts about like a comic
> sergeant-major, concentrating his attacks on copulating
> couples.

A sequel to *Lady Frankenstein* was planned but we
must be thankful that so far it has not materialized.
But there were further sexual adventures ahead for the
Frankenstein Monster in another Italian production
made the following year when Mario Mancini

Baron Frankenstein's creation from *Lady Frankenstein*
(*Condor International/Scotia Barber*)

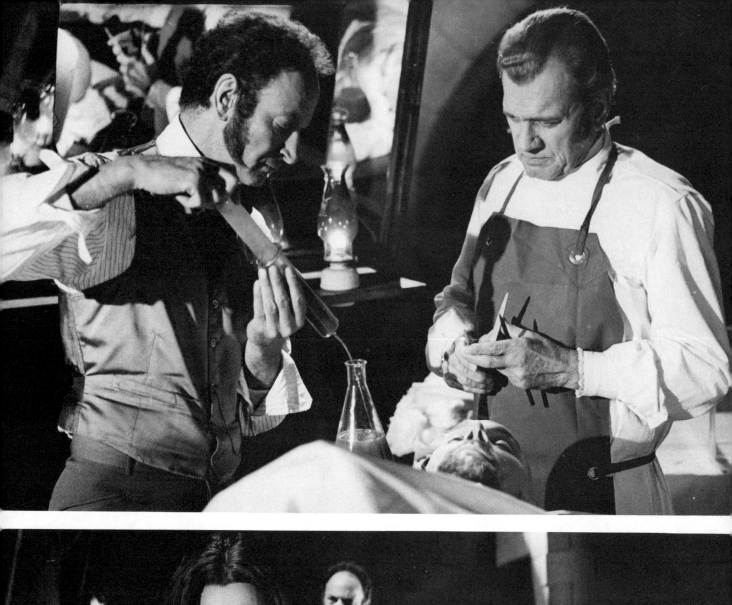

left : Baron Frankenstein (Joseph Cotten) and his assistant in *Lady Frankenstein (Condor International/Scotia Barber)*

opposite below : Tania Frankenstein (Sarah Bay) discovers that her father has been killed by his Monster in *Lady Frankenstein (Condor International/Scotia Barber)*

right : Nudity enters the Frankenstein series as Lady Tania Frankenstein reveals all to her new creation in *Lady Frankenstein (Condor International/Scotia Barber)*

below : Captain Harris, a police inspector (Mickey Hargitay), tracking down clues in *Lady Frankenstein (Condor International/Scotia Barber)*

directed *Frankenstein 1980*, featuring English actor John Richardson, who had made an effective appearance in Mario Bava's vampire classic *Black Sunday* as well as making three films for Hammer. A nude Frankenstein monster was not an appealing idea. However, sex was beginning to play a more important part in continental Frankenstein films.

In 1973 Britain produced what appears to have been a musical horror fantasy called *Son of Dracula*, which had nothing whatsoever to do with Universal's memorable low-budget shocker of 1943. Singer Harry Nilsson played a vampire and also provided the musical score, which was later released by RCA Records. Also in the cast were Ringo Starr and Freddie Jones (who played Professor Frankenstein), while Freddie Francis, who had previously directed *The Evil of Frankenstein* for Hammer, was brought in to take charge of production. But, sad to relate, the film seems to have vanished without trace and without being given a circuit release in Britain.

That same year saw one of the most original and most accomplished films ever to feature the Frankenstein Monster. *The Spirit of the Beehive* was a Spanish production set in a small village on the plains of Castile in 1940. Here, two young children, Ana and Isabel, visit a travelling film show where they see James Whale's *Frankenstein*. They are fascinated by Karloff's Monster, and that night Ana asks her sister if the Monster was really killed. Isabel tells her that the creature is not dead and is in reality a spirit whom anyone can call up. Later Isabel shows Ana a barn where she says the Monster lives, and on the ground is a large footprint. Ana returns to the barn where she meets and befriends a fugitive who is hiding there, but when she pays the man a further visit she finds that he has gone and only a blood stain remains. The girl flees from the scene and takes refuge by a river where she gazes into the water and sees the reflection of the Frankenstein Monster. The child is later discovered in an old ruin having lapsed into a coma. But one night she walks out onto her balcony and announces to whatever is waiting for her: "It is Ana. It is Ana."

right : The Monster (José Villasante) walks again in this rare still from *The Spirit of the Beehive (Contemporary Films)*
below : Ana (Ana Torrent) and the rest of the audience sit entranced as they watch James Whale's *Frankenstein* in *The Spirit of the Beehive (Contemporary Films)*

In *Flesh for Frankenstein* Udo Keir and his assistant bring a fresh look to monster-making *(EMI)*

Director Victor Erice was the guiding light behind this unique film, having conceived the original idea with Angel Fernandez Santos. His cast consisted of non–professionals, some of whom give very sensitive performances, and José Villasante is a more than acceptable Monster. Erice's achievement was truly remarkable, and in many ways he managed to reflect a deep understanding of Mary Shelley's story. Like the Frankenstein Monster, Ana is still coming to terms with a cruel world as a veil of innocence is slowly stripped from her. The press was glowing in its praise. The *Observer* found it "A work of true poetic imagination", while the London *Evening Standard* termed it "A fascinating experience". The trade paper, *Cinema and TV Today*, summed it up:

> Victor Erice has invaded the mind of a child with remarkable success, although the miraculous perform-ances of Ana Torrent and Isabel Telleria are a considerable asset.

The Italians were back in 1973 with a new entry to the series, *House of Freaks*. This time Frankenstein (who had his title changed to Count) was played by none other than Rossano Brazzi, and the film also imported the talents of the venerable J. Carrol Naish in what was to be one of his final performances.

Italy was also the home of the strangest Frankenstein film of the seventies when, in 1973, Andy Warhol and his director Paul Morrissey joined forces with Carlo Ponti to produce two horror films. *Blood for Dracula* featured Udo Keir as the vampiric Count and also misused the talents of Vittorio de Sica and Roman Polanski. Morrissey also wrote the piece, which was liberally laced with sex scenes.

opposite above : A victim is about to lose his head in *Flesh for Frankenstein (EMI)*

opposite below : Joe Dallesandro starred in both of Andy Warhol's horror films. Here he prepares to bring a vampire's life to an end in *Blood for Dracula (EMI)*

Tim Curry and Peter Hinwood as creator and created in
The Rocky Horror Picture Show (20th Century-Fox)

Warhol and Morrissey then decided to turn their attention from Bram Stoker to Mary Shelley. *Flesh for Frankenstein* (also known as *Andy Warhol's Frankenstein*) was an even gorier piece of nonsense. Udo Keir now played Frankenstein and Morrissey delighted in showing surgical operations in great detail. The whole revolting mess fell foul of the British censor who demanded cuts. Morrissey also filmed the production in 3-D and demonstrated that he was no more able to use it successfully than many of the directors of the early fifties. He fell into the old trap of simply pelting the audience with objects, only this time human organs were thrust out of the screen.

In 1975 Jim Sharman brought the highly successful *Rocky Horror Show* to the screen as *The Rocky Horror Picture Show*. The transference to the screen worked extremely well and Tim Curry was able to perform his role of Frank N. Furter for a wider audience. Sharman managed to produce that rare breed of theatrical spin-off: a screen treatment that is faithful to the spirit of the stage show.

Two years later, Calvin Floyd, an American filmmaker, who works mostly in Sweden, set out to tackle the Frankenstein story afresh. His version, made for Aspekt Films of Stockholm, was filmed in Ireland with a cast that included Leon Vitali as Frankenstein, Per Oscarsson as the Monster, and Stacey Dorning as Elizabeth. The film, *Victor Frankenstein*, was screened at the Paris Fantasy Film Festival in the same year and proved to be a faithful rendering of the story, and for the first time part of the action was set in the Orkneys. The script by Floyd and his wife, Yvonne, had much to commend it, but critics, while applauding a return to Mary Shelley, thought that most of the horror in the story had been removed.

The European Frankenstein films have mostly fallen into an obvious trap. They have merely tried to ape the products of America and Britain. In their heyday Hammer were considered to produce extremely gory films, but compared with some of the recent Italian and German productions they appear fairly restrained. Producers seem content to increase the more gory aspects of their films in an attempt to revolt rather than horrify. Blood and sex have replaced style, and the essence of Mary Shelley's myth has been effectively quashed.

8 Down Mexico Way and Further

Frankenstein's cinematic success was not confined to America and Europe. Other parts of the world were ready and willing to present their version of Mary Shelley's saga, although in most cases the original book was left far behind.

Mexico is steeped in superstition and it is not surprising that a fantasy film industry has developed to satisfy the Mexican craving for chills. Indeed Latin America possesses one of the largest fantasy audiences in the world.

In the thirties Universal had made special Spanish-language versions of some of its films. Lugosi's *Dracula* was, however, never seen in Mexico, and instead the Mexicans saw a Spanish version of the film starring Carlos Villarias. This production was filmed on the original Universal sets and directed by George Melford, who had formerly been responsible for "B"-feature westerns. Universal realized that there was a large Mexican audience for this type of entertainment and so did film producers in Mexico.

Mexican horror films are primarily intended for domestic consumption, although they have proved popular in some parts of Europe and North America. Most of the films appear to be made on the slimmest of budgets and are fairly crudely executed. German Robles is the industry's top star and usually plays vampires. But the most outstanding contribution to Mexican horror comes from a masked wrestler called El Santo (The Saint). During the course of a long-running series of films, Santo has been pitted against the Frankenstein Monster, Dracula, Jack the Ripper, assorted vampires and werewolves, aliens from outer space, and even Adolf Hitler. Sometimes the grand finale is even held in the wrestling ring and the films usually descend to the realms of knockabout farce. With such a vast army of villains to fight it is no wonder that Santo occasionally needs help, and he is sometimes joined by another wrestler, Blue Demon. Santo must be the only person ever to have defeated the Frankenstein Monster with a step-over toe hold.

El Castillo de los Monstruos, made in 1957, saw the first Mexican appearance of the Frankenstein Monster. Evangelina Elizondo and popular Mexican comic Clavillazo played a honeymoon couple forced to spend the night in a creepy old castle equipped with the standard trappings of cobwebs, creaking doors, and nocturnal prowlers. Also inhabiting the mansion are Count Dracula, a werewolf, a mummy, a pale imitation of the Creature from the Black Lagoon, and, of course, the Frankenstein Monster. After many feeble chases our hero and heroine escape from the castle. Only German Robles as Count Dracula

was able to bring any style to the proceedings.

In 1961 another comedy horror subject was attempted when Benito Alazraki directed *El Vampiro y Compania*, a loose reworking of the plot of *Abbott and Costello meet Frankenstein*, with a vampire planning to transplant the brain of a dimwit into the skull of the Monster. But his plans are foiled by the Wolfman with whom he fights in the traditional fiery finale, while the Frankenstein Monster sinks into a bog as he had done in *House of Frankenstein*. The film met with a fair degree of success in Latin America and proved that the Mexicans enjoyed laughter with their shivers.

There was a helping of straightforward horror in 1962, however, when Rafael Baledon directed *Orlak, el Infierno de Frankenstein*. This time Frankenstein's creation is called Orlak and sports a metal head, which responds to radio controls. Frankenstein completes his handiwork by providing the creature with an artificial face, but in a neat finale the Monster comes too close to the flames and its face melts.

But the Frankenstein Monster has never encountered an adversary stranger than El Santo, the wrestling super-hero of Mexico. This silver-masked muscleman has been in action on the screen since the early sixties and his exploits seem to have been inspired by the Hercules, Maciste, and Ursus films that were popular in Italy. In Europe Santo has been renamed Superman on many posters.

In 1969 Santo was partnered by fellow wrestler Blue Demon for *Santo y Blue Demon contra los Monstruos*, which was directed by Gilberto Martinez Solares. In this epic, an evil scientist and his assistant capture Blue Demon and subject him to a cloning process to produce an evil double of the wrestler. Not content with this triumph, the scientist revives a whole menagerie of monsters including vampires, a Mummy, a Wolfman, and even a Cyclops. The Monsters then attempt to kidnap Santo's girlfriend. In a hilarious finale Santo meets the Monsters in the wrestling ring and defeats not only them but the false Blue Demon as well. The Frankenstein Monster also receives his just desserts in the wrestling ring. For some reason the make-up department had decided to give the Monster a moustache and beard, which aptly matched the ludicrous plot of the film. Despite these bizarre happenings, the public clamoured for a return match.

In 1971, therefore, both Monster and super-hero took to their respective corners for another round. This time the director, or should one say referee, was Miguel Delgado, and the film was entitled

Santo contra la Hija de Frankenstein. Santo is now pitted against the daughter of the great scientist who, while attempting to discover the secret of eternal youth, has created a super-creature called Ursus. The only surprise is that the Monster is defeated in the early stages of the film, but from then on Santo's adventures are rather mundane as he makes his way through the usual cardboard sets and wooden plot.

The Mexican horror film has occasionally used the imported services of such stalwarts as Lon Chaney Jr, John Carradine, and Boris Karloff, but alas none of these actors has featured in any of the films mentioned in this chapter. The market for these films is limited in North America and hardly any of the Mexican productions have found their way to Britain. They remain a unique, if not very satisfactory, addition to the Frankenstein saga.

If the Frankenstein films of Mexico have a rather dated appearance, the monster films of Japan are geared to the world of the future and science fiction. The Toho Company has been producing monster films since the late fifties, beginning with a giant fire-breathing creature called Godzilla, which went on the rampage and devastated Tokyo. This production was so successful that director Inoshiro Honda and special-effects man Eiji Tsuburaya unleashed a series of outsize monsters, including a bird-like creature called Rodan, a giant moth called Mothra, and a variety of creatures from outer space. Toho has probably lost count of the number of times that Godzilla and his friends have devastated Tokyo and other Japanese towns.

By 1963 the Toho Company had found a profitable market for its products overseas and was beginning co-production deals with foreign producers. In their first venture with America, producer John Beck joined forces with Toho to produce a film that revived one of the screen's great monsters, King Kong, and in *King Kong versus Godzilla* the great ape was pitted against Japan's own superbeast.

Gone were the ingenious animations of Willis O'Brien, the man who had originally brought Kong to life; in their place was a man in a monkey suit. It was a sad affair but it made a lot of money, and Toho, delighted by the results, planned even larger productions. Back in America *Famous Monsters of Filmland* magazine reported that O'Brien's widow had refused to attend the premiere of the film. She stayed at home and shed a few tears for the memory of a once great creation.

Strangely enough, Willis O'Brien had planned a film in which King Kong would have met and done battle with a giant creation of Dr Frankenstein's, but he had not been able to finance the project, and all that remained was a plot outline and a few sketches. It

In *El Castillo de los Monstruos* Evangelina Elizondo is menaced by a Mexican version of the Frankenstein Monster *(Producciones Sotomayor)*

Run for your lives

YMOND BURR
a Cast of Thousands

GODZILLA

Cert **X** ADODULTS ONLY

KING OF THE MONSTERS! *is coming*

Japan's first and most memorable monster, Godzilla, a typical example of far-eastern science fiction *(Toho)*

seemed unlikely that a giant Frankenstein Monster would ever hit the screen until Toho decided that they should embark on a Frankenstein film. To make the film internationally viable, Toho imported American actor Nick Adams for a leading role, and in 1965 work began on *Furankenshutain Tai Baragon*, which was released in English-speaking countries as *Frankenstein Conquers the World*.

Like other Toho productions, the film contained outsize monsters and gave the company's special-effects men plenty of scope. The plot was ingenious, even if the finished result was on the shoddy side.

The film begins at the end of World War II when German scientists, foreseeing an allied victory, ship the heart of the Frankenstein Monster to Hiroshima. With the destruction of the Japanese city, the heart is thought to be lost forever, but years later there are reports of a wild boy who has been seen attacking animals. An American doctor, James Bowen (Nick Adams), seeks out the boy and is startled to discover that he has been created from the heart of the Frankenstein Monster thanks to the effects of radiation from the atomic bomb. But his problems are

just beginning, for the boy is growing rapidly and escapes from his clutches. At the same time a giant reptile called Baragon, which has been revived by a convenient earthquake, goes on the rampage. The army prepares to do battle with the new menace, but the Monster boy intervenes and fights Baragon to the death, but another earthquake brings about a timely end to his adventures as his body vanishes forever.

As a comic-strip Kaoru Mabuchi's script worked fairly well and was obviously intended for a juvenile audience, but the British censor did not agree and gave it an "X" rating. A film like this stands or falls by its special effects, and Eiji Tsuburaya's work was variable in quality. His monsters did not rely on costly animation, and Baragon was obviously a man in a dragon-like suit. Some of the model work was acceptable, some left much to be desired. Inoshiro Honda stage-managed the entire proceedings with his customary flair and brought off a spectacular finale. But ultimately the film remains unsatisfactory.

Somehow the Frankenstein myth does not transfer well to the twentieth century.

Japan planned further Frankenstein films, but none has so far seen the light of day. But if the Japanese have lost interest in the Frankenstein story, other countries have been willing and able to take another stab at it. The film industry in the Philippines has had much help in recent years from the United States and many co-productions have been made.

Harry Paul Harber scripted an unofficial version of H. G. Wells' *The Island of Dr Moreau*, called *Terror is a Man*. Francis Lederer, a fine actor with the unfortunate habit of appearing in less than interesting films, starred as Dr Girard, a Park Avenue surgeon who is experimenting on a lonely island. A young man named Fitzgerald, washed ashore after a shipwreck, is horrified to discover that the doctor has created a man-like creature out of a panther, which needless to say, escapes and, with its master, meets a fitting end.

The production has many ragged edges and is handicapped by some poor supporting performances, but Lederer's performance evokes much sympathy for Girard. The creature itself is not impressive and the limited budget is obvious, but there is a certain commendable honesty about Gerardo De Leon's production and more than a little to admire.

The Frankenstein Monsters of Mexico and Japan have little to offer the Frankenstein myth. The Mexicans have turned the creature into a lumbering buffoon and a target for bad comedy, while the Japanese have reduced him to the level of a comic-strip. At least in the Philippines they have had the decency not to use his name. Perhaps a little respect for Mary Shelley's Monster still exists.

opposite left : The World's largest Frankenstein Monster in the Japanese-produced *Frankenstein Conquers the World* (*Toho*)
below : Nick Adams and a Japanese crowd look on as the giant Frankenstein Monster prepares to do battle in *in Frankenstein Conquers the World* (*Toho*)

AMERICAN INTERNATIONAL PRESENTS
NICK ADAMS
starring in
"FRANKENSTEIN CONQUERS THE WORLD" x
IN COLORSCOPE
FROM ANGLO AMALGAMATED FOR WARNER-PATHE RELEASE

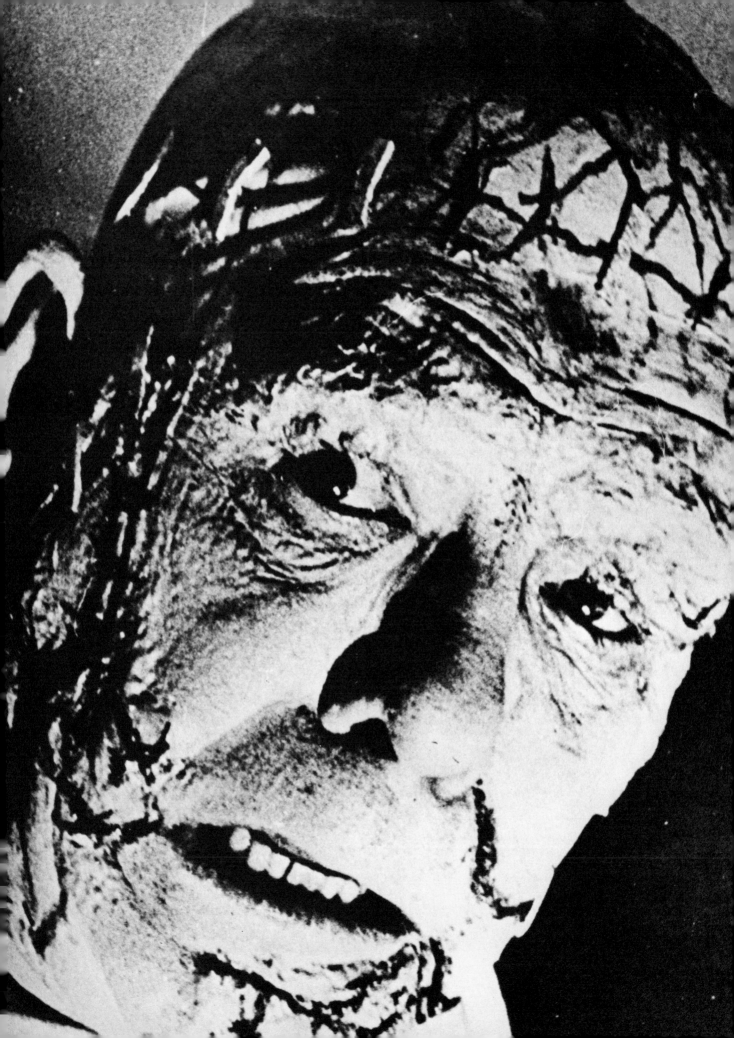

9 The Television Age

By the 1950s television was beginning to exert its stranglehold over the entertainment industry. Producers for the small screen were constantly looking out for new drama subjects, and when they were unable to find them, they returned to tried and tested favourites. It was no surprise, therefore, when the American ABC network turned its attention to the Frankenstein theme.

In 1952 its *Tales of Tomorrow* series featured an adaptation of Frankenstein starring Lon Chaney Jr. The broadcast was live and in black and white. Live television productions usually had their problems and this was no exception—not helped by the fact that a number of the cast has never worked in the medium before. Chaney was forced to spend some four hours in the chair of make-up artist Vincent Kehoe, and, as the time dragged on, he failed to realize that transmission was near. When he walked on to the studio floor he imagined that another rehearsal was taking place and avoided smashing any of the props. After the performance he was astonished to hear that the play had been transmitted. The result was as unsatisfactory as Chaney's make-up—scars covered his forehead and cheeks, and clamps were fixed to the side of his skull—and it was not surprising that television companies left the myth alone for a few years.

By 1957 NBC plucked up the courage to attempt another adaptation, but it confined its production to off-peak time on its *Matinee Theater* show. The Monster this time was the Italian Primo Carnera, a former world heavyweight boxing champion, who was now reduced to bouts of free-style wrestling. The previous year he had acted in a British production, *A Kid for Two Farthings*, in which he had played the villain, and his imposing physique made him a fine choice for the Monster, but his make-up was the usual collection of scars.

NBC's production was the first in colour, but with a running time of only one hour, the plot had to be drastically condensed. The Monster attempts to force the scientist to create a mate for him, but Frankenstein is reluctant and finally fights the creature on the battlements of his castle, with the Monster falling to his death in the finale. This unambitious presentation had a certain honesty about it and, within its own limitations, appears to have worked fairly well.

In 1957 work began on what should have been the most ambitious Frankenstein project ever to grace the small screen. Hammer Films, having made a great success out of its productions for the big screen, was being courted by Columbia Pictures, who offered the British company finance for many of its productions. There were also plans to link the two companies together for a television series.

Tales of Frankenstein was to be made in conjunction with Columbia's Screen Gems television subsidiary. Hammer planned a series based on its Frankenstein feature films, but the American company had other ideas, and after much discussion the pilot episode was shot in Hollywood, with Michael Carreras, the producer, the only member of the Hammer team in attendance.

W. Lee Wilder directed the pilot episode, which was written by Curt Siodmak. The crucial role of Baron Frankenstein was played, not by Peter Cushing, but by the German actor Anton Diffring. For the part of the creature the company selected Don Megowan, whose physique was more than adequate for the part and whose make-up was reminiscent of the Karloff original.

The pilot episode was entitled *The Face in the Tombstone Mirror* but its plot was not original: Baron Frankenstein creates another Monster, but the latest creature has the brain of a man suffering from a deadly illness. The Monster escapes and searches for the widow of the man whose brain he now possesses. This theme was later used in *Frankenstein Must be Destroyed*.

Further episodes in the series were to have included modern stories bearing no resemblance to the Frankenstein theme, but after viewing the pilot episode both sides decided to call it a day and *Tales of Frankenstein* was scrapped. *The Face in the Tombstone Mirror* made fleeting appearances on American screens, but it has yet to be seen in Britain and the rest of the world. Hammer later joined forces with Twentieth Century-Fox for another television series, *Journey to the Unknown*, which was a series of little merit, although an occasional episode sparkled. None of the stories featured Frankenstein or any of the standard horror myths.

The Monster's next television appearance took many American horror fans by surprise. On 26 October 1962 the switchboard at the offices of *Famous Monsters of Filmland* magazine was jammed with calls. The cause of this frenzied activity was the screening by CBS Television of an episode of their *Route 66* series. Most of the callers had missed the start of the episode and were amazed to see the Hunchback of Notre Dame, the Wolfman,

Lon Chaney Jr as the first Frankenstein Monster to appear on television *(ABC TV)*

101

The Addams Family have a reunion *(ABC TV)*

the Mummy, and the Frankenstein Monster all in the same programme. And who should be under the make-up of the Frankenstein Monster? None other than Boris Karloff.

The episode in question was *Lizard's Leg and Owlet's Wing* and concerned a horror convention in Chicago, which was attended by Peter Lorre, Lon Chaney Jr, and Boris Karloff. The terrible trio discuss the monsters they have portrayed on the screen and Karloff suggests that modern audiences are too sophisticated to be scared by such creatures as the Frankenstein Monster. Lorre and Chaney disagree and set out to prove the point by dressing up as their famous creations. Chaney not only revived his two most famous characters, the Wolfman and the Mummy, but he also portrayed his father's role in *The Hunchback of Notre Dame*, while Lorre, with his tongue firmly in his cheek, appeared in a sinister cloak. And Karloff, after 23 years, recreated his most famous role. The episode ends with Karloff's theory being triumphantly demolished.

One of television's weirdest families, the Munsters *(Universal City Studios)*

How Screen Gems ever managed to get Karloff to don the electrodes remains a mystery, but he appears to have enjoyed this entertaining television spoof. Make-up man Ben Lane recreated the Jack Pierce original and came up with a competent result considering the short time he had to produce it.

By 1964 television producers had again fallen back on the old ploy of laughing at once proud monsters. ABC Television presented a comedy series, based on the characters created by cartoonist Charles Addams, *The Addams Family*. This lovable collection of ghouls was led by John Astin as Gomez and Carolyn Jones as his wife, Letitia. Uncle Fester, played by Jackie Coogan, was constantly experimenting in the cellar and his favourite trick was to make an electric light-bulb light up in his mouth. There was also a butler called Lurch, played by a giant of an actor called Ted Cassidy, as well as two children. The family home was a rambling old mansion, which was constantly being visited by other weird relations. A disembodied hand called Thing helped to do most of the housework. The series was a great success and had a certain amount of style. It was also greatly helped by the performances of the regular cast, in particular John Astin and Carolyn Jones.

In the same year CBS produced its own weird family, *The Munsters*. The series was produced by Universal, who decided to model the main characters after its own most famous monsters. Herman Munster was played by Fred Gwynne in a make-up that closely resembled the Jack Pierce Frankenstein Monster. Bud Westmore, head of the Universal make-up department, was responsible for Gwynne's appearance and the result was highly pleasing. Gwynne had previously starred in the successful comedy series *Car 54, Where Are You?* and had developed an easy-going comedy style.

Herman's wife, Lily, was played by Yvonne de Carlo with a suitably pallid complexion and long flowing dresses. Lily's father, who also lived in the Munster home, was a fully fledged vampire and his appearance was obviously modelled on that of Bela Lugosi. He was portrayed by Al Lewis who had also appeared with Gwynne in *Car 54, Where Are You?* The two other regulars in the show were Herman's son, Eddie (Butch Patrick), who had a wolf-like appearance and pointed ears, and the Munster's niece, Marilyn (Beverly Owen), the only normal member of the family. Later Pat Priest took over the role. Marilyn was always pitied by the other members of the Munster family because they thought she was ugly.

The Munsters ran for two years, and at the end of the series Universal decided to put the family in their one and only feature film. It was called *Munster Go Home* and, unlike the series, was filmed in colour. George Tibbles wrote the script in conjunction with producers Joe Conelly and Bob Mosher, and Earl Bellamy directed the proceedings.

When the film was seen in Britain it was released as a second feature and cut by 10 minutes, but when it was later purchased by the Independent Television consortium a complete print was at last screened in the United Kingdom. It was clear that the Munsters had reached the end of their careers. Although it had some funny moments, the film was not a success. In their heyday the Munsters were extremely popular, although the series lacked much of the charm and style of *The Addams Family*, and their shows are constantly being revived on television screens throughout the world. In 1977 HTV, the Independent Television company serving Wales and the West of England, revived the show on Sunday mornings at 11 o'clock and were surprised to see a dramatic rise in the ratings during the programme's half-hour transmission. The Munsters may be gone but they are certainly not forgotten.

By 1968 Britain was ready to attempt a television version of Mary Shelley's novel. Robert Muller joined forces with Thames Television to produce a one-hour adaptation. It was a mostly studio-bound production and starred Ian Holm, as both Victor Frankenstein and his Monster, and Sarah Badel, who played Elizabeth and managed to establish a finer character than most of her predecessors. Muller was forced to pare the plot but he managed to develop his characters beyond the usual stereotypes. Ian Holm was a highly effective Frankenstein and an even more effective Monster, although far removed from the Universal creatures.

Robert Muller claimed, like many other writers who have adapted the story, that he had returned to the original novel. In fact, modifications still had to be made to reduce the plot to an hour-long television play. Later, when Muller had moved to the BBC, he was responsible for another intriguing story based on the Frankenstein myth.

The next televised appearance of the Frankenstein Monster occurred in the same year, when ABC Television in America presented a three-hour version of Mary Shelley's story, in which Frankenstein was played by Robert Foxworth and his creation by Bo Svenson. This highly literate adaptation of the story did not boast a famous cast, but it had much to commend it. The director was Glen Jordan and the producer was Dan Curtis. The supernatural had always been an inspiration to Curtis, whose television feature film *The Night Stalker*, achieved a higher rating than any other televised film of 1972. Later Curtis produced a television version of *Dr Jekyll and Mr Hyde* and even came to Britain to film his own version of *Dracula* with Jack Palance. He obviously cared about classic horror fiction, and it showed in *Frankenstein*. Together with Glenn Jordan and writers Sam Hall and Richard Landau, Curtis created a stimulating production.

But the most ambitious version of the Frankenstein myth was made for NBC Television. As long ago as 1971 Universal had been planning a massive production of *Frankenstein*. This time the studio was determined to return to Mary Shelley's book and include sections that have never been touched on in film or television adaptations. It was an extremely ambitious project and Universal decided that it would entrust the script to the novelist Christopher Isherwood and his collaborator Don Bachardy. There would be a distinguished cast and the film would run for nearly four hours. Isherwood and Bachardy, who were fascinated by the relationship between Frankenstein and the creature and felt that this should be the crux of the whole film, produced an elaborate script.

The authors began to disagree with Universal, especially when the company appointed Jack Smight as director, although Smight was a highly accomplished director of such thrillers as *No Way To Treat A Lady*, and had been responsible for a stylish adaptation of the work of Ray Bradbury in *The Illustrated Man*. The project suffered many delays and finally went into production at Pinewood studios in England in 1973. Meanwhile, a screenwriters' dispute had broken out in Hollywood, and both

Isherwood and Bachardy were forbidden to work while it lasted. They were eventually brought to Britain to rewrite some scenes, but much of the final script was greatly altered by the producers. Isherwood and Bachardy washed their hands of the project and instead insisted on having their screenplay published as a book.

The cast was nearly all British and there were some distinguished names on hand in minor roles. Leonard Whiting played Victor Frankenstein and was supported by James Mason, David McCallum, Sir Ralph Richardson, Sir John Gielgud, Tom Baker, and Jane Seymour. The crucial role of the Monster was played by Michael Sarazzin.

In America NBC broadcast the film in two, two-hour parts, but in Britain Universal decided to distribute it as a cinema feature film. However, in doing so, they made drastic cuts in the running time and the British press gave the truncated film a critical mauling. A year later the BBC purchased the British television rights and screened the complete film at

Grandpa (Al Lewis) and Herman (Fred Gwynne) in the Munsters' only feature film, *Munster Go Home* (*Universal Pictures*)

Christmas. *Frankenstein : The True Story* was not the best of titles for the film, for it certainly wasn't the true story, as reviewers were at pains to point out, but it did restore some important factors from Mary Shelley's novel.

Victor Frankenstein, a newly qualified doctor, attends the funeral of his brother who has been drowned, bemoaning that science is not yet able to restore life to the dead. On his way to Edinburgh, Victor comes upon a ploughboy who has had a serious accident. He takes the boy to a local hospital where another doctor, Henry Clerval, is forced to amputate the boy's arm. Victor is astonished when Clerval collects the limb for further use in his experiments. Fascinated by Clerval's work, Victor joins forces with him as they plan to bring life to a body constructed from corpses. When a quarry accident kills a number of men, Frankenstein and Clerval are soon on the scene to help the injured and collect a few more parts for their experiments. Before their work is complete Clerval dies, leaving Victor to imbue the composite man with life. The experiment appears to be a success and Frankenstein plans to teach his strikingly handsome creation to face the world. But something appears to have gone wrong with his plans, for the new body starts to deteriorate and regress into a Monster. After this initial failure, Frankenstein is visited by Dr Polidori, who has also been experimenting in the same field. Polidori forces Frankenstein to join him in his work so that Frankenstein can operate on Polidori's instructions, the older doctor's hands having been badly damaged. Together they create a female creature, Prima, whom they plan to launch on society. But the jealous creature, who has escaped from Frankenstein's clutches, enters a party where Prima is one of the invited guests and rips her head off.

Polidori and Frankenstein attempt to flee the country on a ship, but the Monster is also on board, and at the height of a storm he goes in search of Polidori. The doctor, who fears thunderstorms, is captured by the creature and hoisted to the top of a mast. Lightning strikes the mast and Polidori is reduced to a skeleton. The ship drifts into the Arctic wastes and Frankenstein and his creation finally perish in an avalanche.

The film offered some first-class performances. Leonard Whiting was an intelligent Frankenstein, while James Mason attacked the role of Dr Polidori with obvious relish. Nicola Pagett gave a fine rendering of Frankenstein's fiancée, Elizabeth, and Jane Seymour was surprisingly effective as Prima. But best of all was Michael Sarrazin who conveyed the pathos of a creature on the path from beauty to ugliness.

The budget for this production was obviously lavish and the art direction was particularly fine, allowing Arthur Ibbetson's camera some splendid compositions. Technically, the film was of a high standard and tautly directed by Jack Smight.

The press in Britain who viewed the 123-minute version in the cinema were not enthusiastic. "How can artists' agents involve their clients in such a mess?" asked London's *Evening Standard*. While the *Guardian* claimed that the film's only distinguishing feature was that: "It has a better class of bit player than any horror movie addict could ask." London's

Michael Sarazzin as the Monster in *Frankenstein: The True Story (Universal City Studios)*

Evening News was even more scathing. "You'll be frightened out of your life, not by the horrors. but at the piling up of inanities", said its disgruntled critic.

But there was a faint note of praise from the *Observer*: "The result is fascinating enough to make it a must for Frankenstein fans" was its critic's verdict. Perhaps it was unfair to screen the film in a medium for which it was not intended, for the complete television print comes as something of a revelation after the abbreviated cinema feature. *Frankenstein: The True Story* remains an absorbing film, and if its promise is not fully realized, there is still much to enjoy in this thoughtful production.

Isherwood and Bachardy had perhaps the last laugh on their producer when the original screenplay was voted the best scenario by the 1976 International Festival of Fantastic and Science Fiction.

In 1977 the Frankenstein theme cropped up once again in a series of late-night dramas presented by BBC Television under the title of *Supernatural*. The stories and the series were the work of Robert Muller, who had earlier been responsible for the Thames Television version of *Frankenstein*. The series featured the Club of the Damned, a group that met at the end of the last century in a house in the Limehouse area of London. They invited to their

meetings those who had bizarre and unusual tales to tell. If the story proved unimpressive, the storyteller might never be seen again, but if his story contained true terror, he was allowed to join the élite members of the club. Robert Muller claimed that his own grandfather was a member of the club. It was not surprising therefore that Muller should return to the Frankenstein theme for one of the stories. The episode was entitled *Heirs* with the subtitle *The Workhouse of Filthy Creation*, and starred Gordon Jackson. The plot was certainly unique.

Howard Lawrence has just completed a book on the life of Shelley and, with his wife Elizabeth and daughter Mary, he attempts to follow in the footsteps of Shelley and Byron in a tour of Europe. In Switzerland they decide to stay at a lonely inn. Lawrence begins to suspect that there is some strange connection between the Villa Diodati and their new lodgings. There appear to be no other guests and strange noises can be heard at night. Lawrence attempts to investigate these nocturnal sounds and is startled to meet a strange old man on the upper floor of the inn. The next day the travellers are told that the

Leonard Whiting as Victor Frankenstein and James Mason as Dr Polidori in *Frankenstein: The True Story (Universal City Studios)*

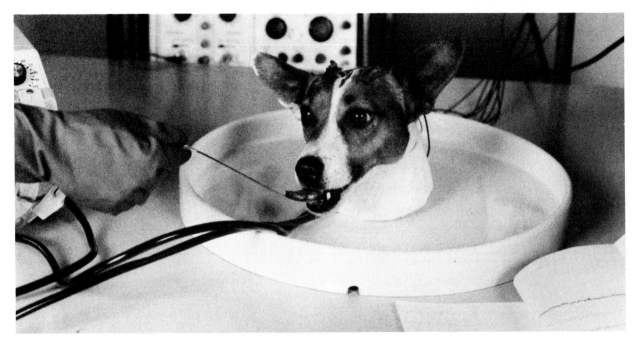

above : The severed head of a dog is kept alive as a preliminary to a major experiment to keep a human brain alive in the *William and Mary* episode of *Tales of the Unexpected*, but *(below)* animal lovers need not worry about how the effect was obtained *(Anglia)*

opposite left : Elaine Stritch examines what is left of her dead husband while Marius Goring looks on. From the *William and Mary* episode of *Tales of the Unexpected (Anglia)*

owners of the inn stage puppet shows for the enjoyment of the locals. That night the puppets, which are life size, perform a terrifying tale in which a magician, who lusts after a young girl, brings to life a figure from a coffin. This strange black creature not only captures the girl for his master, but kills her as well. The magician is grief stricken and stabs the creature to death. To the amazement of the Lawrence family the creature bleeds when it is stabbed. The magician later removes his mask to reveal that he is in reality the inn-keeper. Suddenly Lawrence realizes that Byron and the Shelleys must have witnessed this same puppet show and that the inn-keeper is the model for Frankenstein. Lawrence pays another visit to the upper floor of the inn to discover that the old man is the inn-keeper's father and the manufacturer

of the puppets. His workshop is full of the stench of death and decay. That night the Lawrences are awoken by a noise coming from their daughter's room and Howard is just in time to see his daughter in the arms of the creature from the play.

This episode was perhaps the best of a series that, by and large, was extremely variable in quality. It neatly linked the Frankenstein theme to the Shelleys in a most ingenious way and Gordon Jackson brought strength to the central character of Howard Lawrence. Some highly effective sets and atmospheric lighting made this an acceptable offering for late-night horror lovers.

In 1979 Anglia Television produced an ambitious drama series *Roald Dahl's Tales of the Unexpected*, based on the best-selling author's stories. The series was the brain child of Oscar-winning film producer Sir John Woolf, the guiding hand behind Anglia's drama department, and had a budget of some £1½ million.

One story, *William and Mary*, was closely related to the Frankenstein theme and was adapted for television by Ronald Harwood. Elaine Stritch plays Mary, whose husband, William, has dominated and bullied her for years. But when William dies, Mary discovers he has found a unique way of cheating death. An eminent neurosurgeon, played by Marius Goring, has managed to keep William's brain alive by connecting it to a life-giving machine. The doctor has even managed to connect one of William's eyes to his brain so that he can see. Mary is horrified by the prospect of her husband's continued existence in such a form, but she soon realizes that she can take her revenge on a man who denied her any pleasures. She insists on taking the brain home with her, where she taunts William by forcing him to watch television, which he hated, and delights in blowing smoke into his single eye.

Directed by Donald McWhinnie and produced by John Rosenberg, *William and Mary* was a compact and enjoyable half-hour of black humour with an excellent performance by Marius Goring. It served to prove that half-hour television drama is the ideal format for such stories.

If television has yet to produce a classic version of *Frankenstein* it must be remembered that the medium is still a good deal younger than the cinema, and although its contribution to the myth has so far been limited, recently, as we have seen, producers have been returning to the genesis of Mary Shelley's creation. Perhaps television now has more to offer us for the future than cinema, which has given us so much in the past.

Roald Dahl, author of *William and Mary* and the host of *Tales of the Unexpected (Anglia)*

MONSTER WORLD

JAN. NO. 6   35¢
PDC

HAVE A **COOL YULE** WITH A **GHOUL** IN THIS **HORRIFIC HOLIDAY ISSUE!** PLUS **REVENGE** of the **ZOMBIES** AND **RETURN** of the **VAMPIRE**

10 Short Stories and Novels

If Mary Shelley had lived in the twentieth century, *Frankenstein's* success would have resulted in a publisher demanding a sequel, or a film producer clamouring for the sanctioning of *Frankenstein II*. But Mary never did write a sequel to her first and greatest novel. However, that did not prevent others from exploring the themes that had been fundamental to *Frankenstein*, and since Mary Shelley's death many writers have used her classic as their inspiration. This chapter merely chronicles the more obviously inspired stories, although others have drawn ingenious parallels between Mary Shelley's novel and such diverse works as *Wuthering Heights* and *Moby Dick*.

In 1893 one of the American masters of the short story, Ambrose Bierce, produced one of his finest tales, *Moxon's Master*. The story concerns an engineer who constructs an automaton which can play chess, but when the inventor of the machine sits down to play against his creation he succeeds in beating it. However, the automaton wasn't built to lose and it restores the balance in the game by killing its inventor.

H. G. Wells was another writer who was clearly influenced by the Frankenstein theme. The most obvious expression of this came in *The Island of Dr Moreau*, which he wrote in 1896, a time when his stories were in vogue and his readership was vast. The story of Dr Moreau begins on a lonely Pacific island where a young man finds himself marooned. It happens that the island is the home of Dr Moreau, who has been experimenting with vivisection techniques to produce a race of beast-men. These pitiful creatures have been fashioned from animals brought to the island, and they live in fear of their creator, whose operating theatre is referred to as the "House of Pain". The beast-men are taught to recite a law that Moreau has forced them to live by, but the doctor is unable to prevent a revolt from finally breaking out that results in his death. The castaway manages to escape from the island, leaving behind the last of the beast-men, fully realizing that the creatures will return to a more primitive state, thus destroying Moreau's work.

The Island of Dr Moreau was widely enjoyed even though its theme was extremely controversial, and later Paramount produced a feature film, *Island of Lost Souls*, starring Charles Laughton as Dr Moreau. Laughton neither enjoyed making the film nor the finished result, and the British censor liked it even less and banned it outright.

H. P. Lovecraft was a renowned American author who, to this day, has something approaching a cult following. The first story that Lovecraft succeeded in selling to a publisher was *Herbert West—Re-animator*, which has six different chapters recounting Herbert West's experiments—which would have most certainly brought a gleam of admiration to the eye of Frankenstein.

West is researching into bringing the dead back to life and evolves a fluid that contains animating properties. But his experiments, like those of Frankenstein, have a tendency to go horribly wrong and Herbert West brings to life a whole series of monstrosities. Two of his re-animated corpses turn out to be cannibals and a headless body goes beserk. The creatures eventually mass together and murder the man who has given them life, ripping off West's head.

Lovecraft had obviously put much thought and research into his stories as he discusses such matters as the deterioration of cell tissue in the brain after death. It certainly lends a measure of authenticity that was noticeably lacking in other stories in the genre. Regrettably, Lovecraft did not return to the theme of re-animation. Perhaps he felt that with Herbert West he had explored it sufficiently.

In 1939 *Amazing Stories* published *I, Robot* by Eando Binder. It was the first appearance of one of fiction's most famous robots, Adam Link, the brainchild of Dr Charles Link, who was capable of experiencing human emotions. Adam had to learn his skills in the same way a child does, and it was a long and laborious process. Dr Link dies in an accident and Adam is suspected of the deed. When Adam discovers a copy of *Frankenstein* he deduces that he, himself, has been labelled as a Frankenstein Monster and so sets out to prove to mankind that he is a benevolent creation.

Binder wrote 10 Adam Link stories, all of which proved to be extremely popular. Some of them even found their way into a paperback collection entitled *Adam Link, Robot*. The editions of *Amazing Stories* featuring Adam Link have now become collectors' items.

In 1943 Curt Siodmak, who had written a number of vintage film scripts, wrote his best-selling novel *Donovan's Brain*, which concerned a scientist who was able to keep a dead man's brain alive by connecting it to a life-support machine. But the brain soon starts to exert a strange influence with disastrous consequences. The book was so successful that it spawned three film adaptations. It is strange, therefore, that Siodmak waited until 1968 to produce a sequel, *Hauser's Memory*, in which an experiment involving a memory transplant takes place.

Charles Laughton as Dr Moreau is attacked by the creatures he created from animals in *Island of Lost Souls* (*Paramount*)

So far, the authors and works that we have discussed, although inspired by Mary Shelley's creation, have fought shy of using the name of Frankenstein. But there are some notable exceptions. In the 1950s, French writer Benoit Becker produced six books featuring Boris Karloff's Monster on the covers, but *The Tower of Frankenstein, The Step of Frankenstein, The Night of Frankenstein, The Seal of Frankenstein, Frankenstein Roams,* and *The Cave of Frankenstein* did not feature the Frankenstein Monster.

In 1936 the Readers' Library of Britain published an adaptation of the screenplay of the Universal film *The Bride of Frankenstein*. The novel was written by Michael Egremont, and in later years other authors tackled the same task with other films in the Frankenstein series.

By 1958 the Hammer horror cycle was getting into top gear, and Panther books in Britain decided to cash in on the company's success by issuing a novel version of Jimmy Sangster's screenplay for *The Revenge of Frankenstein*.

In 1965 Harry Harrison decided to take a fresh look at the Frankenstein story with the aptly titled *At Last, the True Story of Frankenstein*. A reporter visits Victor Frankenstein V, who is exhibiting a creature that he claims is the original Frankenstein Monster. As luck would have it, Victor is keen to tell the true story of his ancestor's experiments. It appears that the original Victor Frankenstein was a most misunderstood man who had told his story to Mary Shelley, who had then made a number of crucial modifications to it before writing her novel. Frankenstein had not pieced together a man from corpses, but had been attempting to discover a way of prolonging life. The creature on show was merely a zombie. There was just one small problem: as the present creature was merely an animated corpse, its tissue was continually deteriorating. But Victor Frankenstein V has told his story for a purpose, for the reporter is to become his new creature.

The same year brought another short story of note, this time from Arthur C. Clarke. *Dial F for Frankenstein* was set in a world threatened by a giant electronic brain that has the power to cause other machines to revolt, bringing about worldwide chaos in the process.

Back in the world of true commercialism, Hammer Films joined forces with the Pan publishing company of Britain to produce a paperback collection based on

four of their most successful films. John Burke, an author who was extremely adept at such tasks, adapted the scripts of *The Curse of Frankenstein* and *The Revenge of Frankenstein*, together with *The Gorgon* and *The Curse of the Mummy's Tomb*. The *Hammer Horror Omnibus* was so successful that the following year it spawned a sequel, but alas, the second book contained no Frankenstein material whatsoever.

Kurt Vonnegut Jr entered the Frankenstein stakes in 1968 with a story written in the form of a script and published in *Playboy*. *Fortitude* tells how Dr Norbert Frankenstein falls in love with a female head that he has managed to keep alive by linking it to a life-support system. Frankenstein eventually decides to spend eternity with the object of his affection by having his own head linked up to the same machine. It certainly was a unique form of togetherness.

The most prolific Frankenstein author of the twentieth century is undoubtedly Donald F. Glut. In 1973 he produced an exhaustive work on Mary Shelley's creation entitled *The Frankenstein Legend*, and he is also the author of a brand new series of Frankenstein adventures featuring the Monster.

The first of these books, *Frankenstein Lives Again*, begins where Mary Shelley left off. Dr Burt Winslow, a scientist who appears in a number of Glut's stories, discovers the body of the Frankenstein Monster in the Arctic and revives it in Castle Frankenstein. But the Monster is not happy at being brought back to life and heads for the local woods where he falls under the evil influence of Professor Dartani and his travelling horror show. Winslow eventually dispatches the Monster to a supposed doom from the battlements of Castle Frankenstein.

The next novel in the series, *Terror of Frankenstein*, pitted the Monster against a giant robot, and in *Bones of Frankenstein* Victor Frankenstein himself is brought back to life by a dictator who wishes him to build an army of indestructible monsters. Other novels in the series have confronted the Frankenstein Monster with such notable opponents as Count

No 2
30 pence

THE CURSE OF FRANKENSTEIN featured in...

THE HOUSE OF

HAMMER

TO THE DEVIL—A DAUGHTER

BEHIND THE SCENES
AT HAMMER STUDIOS

INTERVIEW WITH HAMMER'S
MONSTER MAKE-UP KING

THE TEXAS
CHAINSAW MASSACRE

Denis Gifford
looks at HORROR FILMS
OF THE 1930's

ITALIAN MONSTER
MAYHEM

Dracula, a werewolf, a mummy, and a descendant of Dr Henry Jekyll. Glut even managed an ingenious amalgam of Conan Doyle and Mary Shelley in *Frankenstein in the Lost World*, in which Burt Winslow and the Frankenstein Monster are marooned on an African plateau after their plane has crashed. The Monster has to contend with such threats as prehistoric cavemen and a whole range of Neanderthal beasts. Glut has also written a collection of short stories under the title of *Tales of Frankenstein*.

Although the Glut books are based on Mary Shelley's original story, much of their inspiration comes from the Universal horror films of the thirties and forties, and Glut delights in confronting one fiend with another. As recreations of a style of motion picture plot that has sadly vanished, they succeed admirably and have proved extremely popular.

In 1973 science-fiction author Brian Aldiss had the ingenious idea of linking the Frankenstein myth and Mary Shelley's Swiss summer in an enterprising way. *Frankenstein Unbound* begins in the year 2020, in a world plagued by time warps and disappearing people. Joe Bodenland becomes a reluctant time-traveller when he finds himself spirited to Switzerland in the summer of 1816. He is staggered to find himself in a world where fact and fiction intermingle, so that he meets not only the Shelleys and Lord Byron, but also Victor Frankenstein and his creature. Bodenland is fascinated by this strange situation and finds himself falling in love with Mary Shelley. He is even invited to share in the conversation with the Shelleys, Byron, and Polidori at the Villa Diodati. He also witnesses the unfolding of the Frankenstein story, and in a gripping finale confronts the Monster in an icy wilderness.

With its parallel story lines, *Frankenstein Unbound* represents a fascinating insight into the Frankenstein story. Aldiss has obviously done a vast amount of research, which has paid off, for the characters of the Shelleys and Byron are magnificently drawn, while Frankenstein himself has such a well-developed personality that he can exist side by side with real-life characters. Aldiss has not only managed to bring a welcome touch of originality to the Frankenstein theme, but has also managed to relate fantasy to reality with great success.

A more formal approach to the theme was offered in *The Cross of Frankenstein*, written in 1975 by Robert J. Myers. It represents a continuation of Mary Shelley's original story and concerns a descendant of the Frankenstein family. Victor Frankenstein is given a package containing letters from his father concerning experiments in the development of a creature. He discovers that his father met with disaster and later begins to wonder whether or not the Monster is actually dead. An American visits Victor in London in the hope that Frankenstein can recreate a synthetic blood that was originally used in the animating of the Monster. Victor is captured and taken to America where he is forced to revitalize his father's creature, who hopes to lead an army of re-animated corpses. Luckily Frankenstein manages to escape from his captors, and the Monster, in a thrilling chase, is swept to the bottom of a river.

Myers' book was a tasteful pastiche of the Frankenstein story and was successful, being published at a time when authors were bringing such characters as Sherlock Holmes out of cold storage for new adventures. The following year Myers brought out a sequel, *The Slaves of Frankenstein*, in which the Monster was partnered by such real-life characters as Robert E. Lee, John Wilkes Booth, and John Brown.

Other recent adventures have included *The Frankenstein Wheel* by Paul W. Fairman and *The Frankenstein Factory* by Edward Hoch. Some excellent short stories on the Frankenstein theme are to be found in Michel Parry's interesting anthology *The Rivals of Frankenstein*, which was published in Britain by Corgi Books in 1977.

The cinema has for some years been providing material for authors and publishers. In 1975 Gilbert Pearlman adapted Gene Wilder and Mel Brooks' script for *Young Frankenstein* into a paperback book, which was published by Star. But the best cinema souvenir came from film historian Richard J. Anobile who, with the help of 1000 frame blow-ups, produced an illustrated version of James Whale's 1931 classic.

It seems that the adventures of the Frankenstein Monster will continue on the printed page for many years to come, for the theme is as fascinating today as it was in that summer of 1816. The later Frankenstein stories have proved that authors are not only striving to give the theme new life, but are attempting a greater understanding of Mary Shelley and the creation of her novel. Derek Marlowe's *A Single Summer with L. B.* and Anne Edwards' *Haunted Summer*, for example, present highly successful attempts at fictionalized accounts of events in the summer of 1816. Perhaps they say more about the Frankenstein myth than many of the stories that bear that illustrious name. It is comforting to know that in the latter part of the twentieth century, Mary Shelley is remembered as well as the Monster that she and Victor Frankenstein created.

The magnificent cover of the second issue of *The House of Hammer* features a scene from *The Curse of Frankenstein* (*Marvel*)

FRANKENSTEIN LOSES HIS PANTS !

This 14-inch high battery operated **FRANKENSTEIN MONSTER** stands on his tombstone, hands outstretched. Turn the switch and he **STARTS TO MOVE!!** His face is a hideous green; his hands and arms claw the air! He grunts and groans!! He is going to attack!!! WOW! Look what happened! **HIS PANTS FALL DOWN**—revealing his red and white underwear shorts—and the

Monster blushes a bright red, changes his mind, and shuts off automatically. Uses ordinary flashlight batteries. The funniest sight you ever saw! Only $5.95 plus 75c for postage & handling.

CAPTAIN COMPANY, BOX 6573, Dept. MO-27, PHILADELPHIA 38, PENNA.

The Captain Company offers a new Frankenstein toy

Conclusion

Frankenstein and his Monster have come a long way since the summer of 1816. Mary Shelley would certainly have been startled to discover that her creation had been turned into a highly commercialized industry.

The Monster has not just appeared in plays, films, books, and television programmes. He has been featured in comic-strips, and Marvel Comics have even given him his very own magazine. The youth market has certainly taken to the creature.

It is now possible to build a plastic model of the Monster, paint him with the help of numbers in a special kit, and play a board game in which the Monster stalks his victims. You can even scare your friends by donning a Frankenstein face-mask designed by Don Post Studios.

The film collector can buy 8 mm versions of the classic Frankenstein films that have been cut down from the Universal originals. Record collectors can even hear Boris Karloff's Monster speak the only words he ever uttered in a record entitled *An Evening with Boris Karloff and His Friends*.

Like the Monster, the story of Frankenstein seems to be immortal. The thunder and lightning that helped to inspire Mary Shelley in 1816 brought forth not just a Monster, but a rich vein of fantasy that, it is hoped, will be successfully mined for many years to come. Even science, which appears to be catching up with Frankenstein, has not diminished the interest shown in the tale. Perhaps it has even increased it. Could the story of Frankenstein be moving from fantasy to reality? Only the future can tell.

Filmography

1910
Frankenstein (USA: Edison Company)
Director: J. Searle Dawley
Cast: Charles Ogle (as the Monster)
(No prints are available)

1914
Der Golem (Germany: Bioscop)
Directors: Paul Wegener, Henrik Galeen
Cast: Paul Wegener, Lyda Salmonova, Henrik Galeen
(Only an incomplete print survives of this, Wegener's first appearance as the stone giant)

1915
Life Without Soul (USA: Ocean Film Corporation)
Director: Joseph W. Smiley
Cast: Percy Darrell Standing, Lucy Cotton, William W. Cohill
(No prints are available)

1916
Homunculus (Germany: Bioscop)
Director: Otto Rippert
Cast: Olaf Fonss, Frederich Kuhn, Theodor Loos
(A serial in six, one-hour chapters)

1917
Der Golem und die Tanzerin (Germany: Bioscop)
Director: Paul Wegener
Cast: Paul Wegener
(No prints are available)

1919
Das Kabinett des Dr Caligari (Germany: Decla-Bioscop)
Director: Robert Wiene
Cast: Werner Krauss, Conrad Veidt, Lil Dagover
(One of the landmarks in the history of the cinema)

1920
Der Golem (Germany: UFA)
Directors: Paul Wegener, Carl Boese
Cast: Paul Wegener, Lyda Salmonova, Albert Steinruck
(Wegener's remake of his 1914 production; still the finest version of the Golem legend)

Il Monstro di Frankenstein (Italy)
Director: Eugenio Testa
Cast: Luciano Albertini, Umberto Guarracino
(No prints are available)

1926
Metropolis (Germany: UFA)
Director: Fritz Lang
Cast: Alfred Abel, Brigitte Helm, Gustave Froehlich
(Contains one of the screen's most impressive robots)

1931
Frankenstein (USA: Universal)
Director: James Whale
Cast: Colin Clive, Boris Karloff, Mae Clarke, Edward Van Sloan, Dwight Frye
(Universal's first excursion into Mary Shelley's tale and perhaps the most successful Frankenstein film)

1935
The Bride of Frankenstein (USA: Universal)
Director: James Whale
Cast: Colin Clive, Boris Karloff, Valerie Hobson, Ernest Thesiger, Elsa Lanchester
(Considered by many to be the finest fantasy film ever made)

1936
Le Golem (Czechoslovakia/France: A.B. Film-Metropolis Pictures)
Director: Julien Duvivier
Cast: Harry Baur, Roger Karl, Gaston Jacquet

1939
Son of Frankenstein (USA: Universal)
Director: Rowland V. Lee
Cast: Boris Karloff, Basil Rathbone, Bela Lugosi, Lionel Atwill, Josephine Hutchinson
(Karloff's last feature film appearance as the Monster)

1942
The Ghost of Frankenstein (USA: Universal)
Director: Erle C. Kenton
Cast: Sir Cedric Hardwicke, Bela Lugosi, Lon Chaney Jr, Ralph Bellamy, Evelyn Ankers, Lionel Atwill
(Lon Chaney Jr dons the electrodes to little effect)

1943
Frankenstein meets the Wolfman (USA: Universal)
Director: Roy William Neill
Cast: Patric Knowles, Ilona Massey, Lon Chaney Jr. Bela Lugosi, Maria Ouspenskaya, Lionel Atwill
(Lugosi's one and only disastrous appearance as the Monster)

1944
House of Frankenstein (USA: Universal)
Director: Erle C. Kenton
Cast: Boris Karloff, John Carradine, Lon Chaney Jr, J. Carrol Naish, George Zucco, Lionel Atwill, Glenn Strange
(Dracula, the Wolfman and the Monster meet for the first time)

1945
House of Dracula (USA: Universal)
Director: Erle C. Kenton
Cast: Lon Chaney Jr, John Carradine, Onslow Stevens, Lionel Atwill, Martha O'Driscoll, Glenn Strange
(Another monster reunion)

1948
Abbot and Costello meet Frankenstein (USA: Universal)
(UK title: *Abbot and Costello meet the Ghosts*)
Director: Charles Barton
Cast: Bud Abbott, Lou Costello, Bela Lugosi, Lon Chaney Jr, Glenn Strange, Lenore Aubert
(The end of the line for the Universal Monsters)

1952
Torticola contre Frankensberg (France)
Director: Paul Paviot
Cast: Roger Blin, Vera Norman, Michel Piccoli

1957

The Curse of Frankenstein (UK: Hammer)
Director: Terence Fisher
Cast: Peter Cushing, Hazel Court, Robert Urquhart,
Christopher Lee
(The first Hammer Frankenstein)

Man without a Body (UK: Eros)
Directors: W. Lee Wilder, Charles Saunders
Cast: Robert Hutton, George Coulouris

El Castillo de los Monstruos (Mexico: Producciones Sotomayor)
Director: Julian Soler
Cast: German Robles, Clavillazo, Evangelina Elizondo

I was a Teenage Frankenstein (USA: American International)
(UK title: *Teenage Frankenstein*)
Director: Herbert L. Strock
Cast: Whit Bissell, Gary Conway, Phyllis Coates

1958

The Revenge of Frankenstein (UK: Hammer)
Director: Terence Fisher
Cast: Peter Cushing, Francis Matthews, Michael Gwynn,
Eunice Gayson

Frankenstein 1970 (USA: Allied Artists)
Director: Howard W. Koch
Cast: Boris Karloff, Rudolph Anders, Mike Lane

Frankenstein's Daughter (USA: Astor Pictures)
Director: Richard Cunha
Cast: Donald Murphy, Susan Knight, John Ashley
(Possibly the worst Frankenstein film ever made)

How to Make a Monster (USA: American International)
Director: Herbert L. Strock
Cast: Robert H. Harris, Gary Conway, John Ashley

The Colossus of New York (USA: Paramount)
Director: Eugene Lourie
Cast: Otto Kruger, Ross Martin, Ed Wolff, Charles Herbert

1959

Die Nackte und der Satan (West Germany: Rapid/Wolfgang
Hartwig/Prisma/Trans Lux)
(US and UK title: *The Head*)
Director:
Cast: Michel Simon, Horst Frank

Terror is a Man (Philippines/USA: Premier Productions/
Lynn-Romero)
Director: Gerardo de Leon
Cast: Francis Lederer, Greta Thyssen, Richard Derr

1960

Doctor Blood's Coffin (UK: Caralan — United Artists)
Director: Sidney J. Furie
Cast: Kieron Moore, Hazel Court

1961

El Vampiro y Compania (Mexico: Cinematografica Calderon)
Director: Benito Alazraki
Cast: Manuel Valdes, Martha Elena Cervantes

1962

House on Bare Mountain (USA: Olympic International Films)

Director: R. Lee Frost
Cast: Bob Cresse, Warren Ames, Jeffrey Smithers

The Cabinet of Dr Caligari (USA: 20th Century-Fox)
Director: Roger Kay
Cast: Glynis Johns, Dan O'Herlihy, Lawrence Dobkin
(Dreadful remake; even author Robert Bloch disowns this one)

Twice Told Tales (USA: Admiral)
Director: Sidney Salkow
Cast: Vincent Price, Sebastian Cabot

Orlak, el Infierno de Frankenstein (Mexico: Filmadora
Independiente)
Director: Rafael Baledon
Cast:

1964

Angelic Frankenstein (USA: Athletic Models' Guild)
Director: Bob Mizer
Cast: They wished to remain anonymous

El Testamento del Frankenstein (Spain)
Director: José Luis Madrid
Cast: Gerard Landry, George Vallis

The Evil of Frankenstein (UK: Hammer)
Director: Freddie Francis
Cast: Peter Cushing, Sandor Eles, Katy Wild, Peter
Woodthorpe, Kiwi Kingston

1965

Fanny Hill meets Dr Erotico (USA)
Director: Barry Mahon
Cast:

Jesse James meets Frankenstein's Daughter (USA: Circle
Productions)
Director: William Beaudine
Cast: John Lupton, Cal Bolder, Narda Onyx
(The Monster's first and last trip west)

Frankenstein meets the Space Monster (USA: Futurama
Entertainment Corporation)
(UK title: *Duel of the Space Monsters*)
Director: Robert Gaffney
Cast: Robert Reilly, James Karen, Nancy Marshall

Furankenshutain Tai Baragon (Japan: Toho)
(US and UK title: *Frankenstein Conquers the World*)
Director: Inoshiro Honda
Cast: Nick Adams, Tadao Takashima

1966

Frankenstein Created Woman (UK: Hammer)
Director: Terence Fisher
Cast: Peter Cushing, Susan Denberg, Barry Warren, Duncan
Lamont

Munster Go Home (USA: Universal)
Director: Earl Bellamy
Cast: Fred Gwynne, Yvonne de Carlo, Al Lewis,
Terry-Thomas
(A spin-off from the successful TV show)

Carry on Screaming (UK: Associated British Pathé)
Director: Gerald Thomas
Cast: Harry H. Corbett, Kenneth Williams, Jim Dale

It (UK: Goldstar)
Director: Herbert J. Leger
Cast: Roddy McDowall, Jill Haworth, Paul Maxwell

1968
La Marca del Hombre Lobo (Spain: Maxper)
(US title: *Frankenstein's Bloody Terror;* UK title: *Hell's Creatures*)
Director: Enrique L. Equiliz
Cast: Paul Naschy, Dianki, Zurakowska
(No sign of the Baron or his Monster)

1969
Frankenstein Must be Destroyed (UK: Hammer)
Director: Terence Fisher
Cast: Peter Cushing, Veronica Carlson, Simon Ward, Freddie Jones

Santo y Blue Demon contra los Monstruos (Mexico: Cinematografica)
Director: Gilberto Martinez Solares
Cast: Carlos Ancira, David Alvizu

Flick (Canada: Agincourt Productions)
(UK title: *Frankenstein on Campus*)
Director: Gil Taylor
Cast: Robin Ward, Kathleen Sawyer

The Forbin Project (USA: Universal)
Director: Joseph Sargent
Cast: Eric Braeden, Susan Clark, Gordon Pinsent

1970
Horror of Frankenstein (UK: Hammer)
Director: Jimmy Sangster
Cast: Ralph Bates, Veronica Carlson, Dennis Price

El Hombre que Vino Ummo (Spain/West Germany/Italy: Producciones Jaime Prades/Eichberg Film/International Jaguar)
(US and UK title: *Dracula versus Frankenstein*)
Director: Tulio Demichelli
Cast: Michael Rennie, Paul Naschy, Karin Dor, Craig Hill

1971
Dracula versus Frankenstein (USA: Independent International Films)
(UK title: *Blood of Frankenstein*)
Director: Al Adamson
Cast: J. Carrol Naish, Lon Chaney Jr, John Bloom

Dracula contra el Dr Frankenstein (Spain)
Director: Jesus Franco
Cast: Howard Vernon, Dennis Price, Fernando Bilbao

Santo contra la Hija de Frankenstein (Mexico)
Director: Miguel M. Delgado
Cast:

1972
La Figlia di Frankenstein (Italy: Condor International)
(US and UK title: *Lady Frankenstein*)
Director: Mel Welles (Ernst Von Theumer)
Cast: Joseph Cotten, Sarah Bay, Mickey Hargitay

Frankenstein 1980 (Italy)
Director: Mario Mancini
Cast: John Richardson, Renato Roman

Frankenstein and the Monster from Hell (UK: Hammer)
Director: Terence Fisher
Cast: Peter Cushing, Shane Briant, Dave Prowse

1973
Son of Dracula (UK)
Director: Freddie Francis
Cast: Harry Nilsson, Ringo Starr, Freddie Jones

House of Freaks (Italy)
Director: Robert Oliver
Cast: Rossano Brazzi, J. Carrol Naish

The Spirit of the Beehive (Spain)
Director: Victor Erice
Cast: Ana Torrent, Isabel Telleria, José Villasante

1974
Flesh for Frankenstein (Italy/USA: Carlo Ponti/Andrew Braunsberg/Jean-Pierre Rassam)
(US title: *Andy Warhol's Frankenstein*)
Director: Paul Morrissey
Cast: Udo Keir, Joe Dalessandro

Blackenstein (USA)
Director: William A. Levey
Cast: John Hart

1975
Young Frankenstein (USA: 20th Century-Fox)
Director: Mel Brooks
Cast: Gene Wilder, Marty Feldman, Peter Boyle

The Rocky Horror Picture Show (UK: 20th Century-Fox)
Director: Jim Sharman
Cast: Tim Curry, Charles Gray, Peter Hinwood

1976
Frankenstein Italian-Style (Italy)
Director: Armando Crispino
Cast: Aldo Maccione

1977
Victor Frankenstein (Sweden/Eire)
Director: Calvin Floyd
Cast: Leon Vitali, Stacey Dorning, Nicholas Clay, Per Oscarsson

Bibliography

Ackerman, Forrest J. (editor), *The Best of Famous Monsters*, Paperback Library Inc., 1965
——, *Famous Monsters Strike Back*, Paperback Library Inc., 1965
——, *The Frankenscience Monster*, Ace, 1969
——, *Son of Famous Monsters*, Paperback Library Inc., 1965
Barbour, Alan G., *A Thousand and One Delights*, Collier-Macmillan, London, 1972
Bigland, Eileen, *Mary Shelley*, Cassell, London, 1959
Brosnan, John, *Movie Magic*, Macdonald, London, 1974
Clarens, Carlos, *Horror Movies*, Secker and Warburg, London, 1968
Dowden, Edward, *The Life of Percy Bysshe Shelley* (2 volumes), Kegan Paul, Trench & Co., London, 1966
Eyles, Allen; Adkinson, Robert; Fry, Nicholas (editors), *The House of Horror*, Lorrimer, London, 1973
Florescu, Radu, *In Search of Frankenstein*, New English Library, London, 1977
Frank, Alan, *Horror Films*, Hamlyn, London, 1977
——, *Monsters and Vampires*, Octopus Books, London, 1976
French, Philip, *The Movie Moguls*, Weidenfeld and Nicolson, London, 1969
Gifford, Denis, *Karloff the Man, the Monster, the Movies*, Curtis Books, New York, 1973
Glut, Donald, *The Frankenstein Legend*, Scarecrow Press, Metuchen N.J., 1973
Halliwell, Leslie, *The Filmgoer's Companion*, Hart-Davis, London, 1977
Halliwell, Leslie, *Film Guide*, Hart-Davis, London, 1977
Holmes, Richard, *Shelley, the Pursuit*, Quartet Books, London, 1976
Ludlam, Harry, *A Biography of Bram Stoker*, New English Library, London, 1977
Nicoll, Allardyce, *A History of English Drama* (6 volumes), Cambirdge University Press, 1959
——, *World Drama*, Harrap, London, 1976
Pattison, Barrie, *The Seal of Dracula*, Lorrimer, London, 1975
Pirie, David, *A Heritage of Horror*, Gordon Fraser, London, 1973
Scheuer, Steven H. (editor), *Movies on TV*, Bantam Books, London, 1977
Shipman, David, *The Great Movie Stars: The Golden Years*, Hamlyn, London, 1970
——, *The Great Movie Stars: The International Years*, Angus and Robertson, London, 1972
Strick, Philip, *Science Fiction Movies*, Octopus Books, London, 1976
Trevelyan, John, *What the Censor Saw*, Michael Joseph, London, 1973

Magazines

Castle of Frankenstein, Famous Monsters of Filmland, Fantastic Monsters of the Films, Films and Filming, Films Illustrated, Horror Monsters, House of Hammer, Journal of Frankenstein, Mad Monsters, Midi-Minuit Fantastique, Modern Monsters, Monthly Film Bulletin, Monster World, Shriek, Sight and Sound, Spacemen, Starburst, Supernatural Filming and *World Famous Creatures.*

Acknowledgements

A book is hardly ever the product of one person and this one is no exception. A number of people and organizations have inspired and aided its creation and to them I wish to offer my sincere thanks. Paul Barnett and Judy and Paul Begg conceived the original project. Leslie Halliwell, whose *Filmgoer's Companion* was never far from my side, gave valuable advice and helped in my search for some elusive stills, as did Don Gale of MCA TV. The staff of the British Film Institute's stills department did some splendid work in locating some rare photographs that I despaired of ever finding. Malcolm Hall offered photographic assistance and advice, while the stills department of Anglia Television provided additional photographs. Peter Cushing was kind enough to spend some time recalling the great days of Hammer horror and was as courteous and charming as I had always imagined him to be. But most of all my thanks go to the men and women who figure in these pages and to Mary Shelley, without whom I would have been at a loss for words.

Index

Abbott and Costello meet Frankenstein, 47, 48, 95
Abbott, Bud, 47, 48
ABC Television, 101, 103, 104
Abominable Snowman, The, 49
Ackerman, Forrest J., 79
Adam Link, Robot, 113
Adams, Nick, 97
Addams, Charles, 103
Addams Family, The, 102, 103, 104
Aldiss, Brian, 117
Allman, Sheldon, 18
All Quiet on the Western Front, 30
American International Pictures, 65, 79, 80
Angelic Frankenstein, 73
Anglia Television, 111
Anobile, Richard J., 117
Asher, Jack, 53
Ashton, Roy, 54
Aspekt Films, 94
Astin, John, 103, 104
Athletic Models' Guild, 73
At Last, the True Story of Frankenstein, 114
Atwill, Lionel, 37, 38, 40, 44

Bachardy, Don, 104, 105, 107
Badel, Sarah, 104
Baker, Tom, 105
Balderston, John L., 32
Bates, Ralph, 57, 59, 60
Batt, Bert, 56
Bava, Mario, 90
Bay, Sarah, 88, 89
BBC Television, 49, 104, 107
Beaudine, William, 73
Beck, John, 96
Becker, Benoit, 114
Bellamy, Earl, 104
Bellamy, Ralph, 40
Bierce, Ambrose, 113
Billy the Kid versus Dracula, 73
Binder, Eando, 113
Biograph Company, 19
Blackenstein, 80
Black Sunday, 90
Blackwood, Algernon, 9
Blackwood's Edinburgh Magazine, 14
Blacula, 80
Blazing Saddles, 80
Bloch, Robert, 73
Blood for Dracula, 92, 93
Blood Seekers, The, see *Dracula versus Frankenstein*
Bloom, John, 79
Boese, Carl, 23
Bonanza, 65
Bones of Frankenstein, 115
Boyle, Peter, 80, 81
Bradbury, Ray, 104

Brazzi, Rossano, 92
Brent, George, 49
Briant, Shane, 62, 63
Bride of Frankenstein, The, 9, 32, 33, 34, 35, 54, 56, 81, 114
Brooks, Mel, 80, 81, 117
Browning, Tod, 27
Brynner, Yul, 79
Burke, John, 115
Byron, Lord George, 11, 12, 117

Cabinet of Dr Caligari, The
    1919 version, 21, 22, 23, 83
    1962 version, 70, 73
Cabot, Sebastian, 73, 74
Captain Company, 118
Car 54, Where are You?, 104
Carlson, Veronica, 60
Carnera, Primo, 101
Carradine, John, 32, 43, 44, 47, 96
Carreras, Michael, 101
Carry on Screaming, 83
Cassidy, Ted, 103
Castillo de los Monstruous, El, 95, 96
Cave of Frankenstein, The, 114
CBS Television, 101, 104
Chaney, Lon, 26, 27
Chaney Jr, Lon, 40, 41, 42, 44, 46, 47, 79, 96, 100, 101, 103
Chrichton, Michael, 79
Christabel, 11, 12
Circle Productions, 73
Claremont, Claire, 11
Clark, Mae, 27
Clarke, Arthur C., 114
Clive, Colin, 27, 30, 32, 35, 81
Cohen, Herman, 65, 67
Cohill, William, 19
Colossus of New York, The, 70, 72
Columbia Pictures Corporation, 51, 101
Comedy Theatre, London, 18
Conelly, Joe, 104
Conway, Gary, 66, 67
Coogan, Jackie, 103
Cooke, Thomas Potter, 15
Corbett, Harry H., 83
Coronet Theatre, Hollywood, 18
Costello, Lou, 47, 48
Cotten, Joseph, 86, 87, 88
Coulouris, George, 83
Count of Monte Cristo, The, 37
Court, Hazel, 49
Cross of Frankenstein, The, 117
Curry, Tim, 18, 94
Curse of Frankenstein, The, 49, 51, 52, 53, 61, 115, 116
Curse of the Mummy's Tomb, The, 115
Curtis, Dan, 104
Cushing, Peter, 49, 50, 52, 54, 55, 56, 57, 58, 59, 61, 63, 101

Dagover, Lil, 23
Dahl, Roald, 110, 111
Dale, Jim, 83
Dallesandro, Joe, 92, 93
Darwin, Erasmus, 12
Davis, Bette, 27
Dawley, J. Searle, 19
Deane, Hamilton, 17, 18
De Carlo, Yvonne, 46, 104
De Leon, Gerardo, 99
Demichelli, Tulio, 85

Denberg, Susan, 56
De Sica, Vittorio, 92
Dial F for Frankenstein, 114
Diffring, Anton, 101
Dobkin, Lawrence, 73
Dr Blood's Coffin, 83, 84
Dr Heidegger's Experiment, 73
Dr Jekyll and Mr Hyde,
    1908 version, 19
    TV version, 104
Donlevy, Brian, 49
Donovan's Brain, 113, 115
Don Post Studios, 119
Dorning, Stacey, 94
Dracula
    Play, 17, 18
    1931 version, 9, 27, 28, 38
    1958 version, 51
    TV version, 104
Dracula contra el Dr Frankenstein, 86
Dracula versus Frankenstein (The Blood Seekers), 79
Duel of the Space Monsters, see *Frankenstein meets the Space Monster*
Dunagan, Donnie, 38

Edinburgh Review, The, 14
Edison, Arthur, 30
Edison Company, 19
Edwards, Anne, 117
Egremont, Michael, 114
Elder, John, *see* Hinds, Anthony
Elizondo, Evangelina, 96
Empire Theatre, Preston, 17
Equiliz, Enrique L., 84
Erice, Victor, 92
Eros Films, 83
Evening with Boris Karloff and his Friends, An, 119
Evil of Frankenstein, The, 54, 55, 56, 90

Face in the Tombstone Mirror, The, 101
Fairman, Paul W., 117
Famous Monsters of Filmland, 8, 9, 79, 96, 101
Fanny Hill meets Dr Erotico, 73
Fanny Hill meets Lady Chatterley, 73
Fantasmagoriana, 11
Farren, Nellie, 15
Feldman, Marty, 81
Figlia di Frankenstein, La (Lady Frankenstein), 86, 87, 88, 89
Fisher, Terence, 49, 53, 55, 56, 62, 83
Flesh for Frankenstein, 92, 93, 94
Flick (Frankenstein on Campus), 78
Florey, Robert, 27
Floyd, Calvin, 94
Fonda, Peter, 79
Fonss, Olaf, 20, 21
Forbin Project, The, 78, 79
Fortitude, 115
Foxworth, Robert, 104
Francis, Freddie, 55, 90
Franco, Jesus, 86
Frank, Horst, 83
Frankenstein
    1910 version, 19, 20
    1931 version, 9, 23, 27, 31, 38, 90
    ABC TV version, 104
    Thames TV version, 104
Frankenstein Conquers the World, see *Furankenshutan Tai Baragon*

Frankenstein Created Woman, 55, 56
Frankenstein Factory, The, 117
Frankenstein in the Lost World, 117
Frankenstein Legend, The, 115
Frankenstein Lives Again, 115
Frankenstein Meets the Space Monster (Duel of the Space Monsters), 78
Frankenstein Meets the Wolfman, 9, 42
Frankenstein Must be Destroyed, 56, 58, 59, 101
Frankenstein 1980, 90
Frankenstein 1970, 65, 69, 70
Frankenstein on Campus, see *Flick*
Frankenstein; or The Demon of Switzerland, 15
Frankenstein's Bloody Terror, see *Marca del Hombre Lobo, La*
Frankenstein's Daughter, 9, 65, 71
Frankenstein: The True Story, 104, 105, 106, 107
Frankenstein Unbound, 117
Frankenstein Wheel, The, 117
Fulton, John P., 47
Furankenshutain Tai Baragon (Frankenstein Conquers the World), 97, 98, 99
Furie, Sidney J., 83
Frye, Dwight, 32

Gaiety Theatre, London, 15
Galeen, Henrik, 20
Genuine, 21
Ghost of Frankenstein, The, 32, 40, 41, 42, 47
Gielgud, Sir John, 105
Glut, Donald F., 115, 117
Godwin, William, 11
Godzilla, 96, 97
Golem, Der
    1914 version, 20
    1920 version, 21, 23
Golem, Le, 84
Golem und die Tanzerin, Der, 20
Gorgon, The, 115
Goring, Marius, 108, 109, 111
Gwynn, Michael, 53, 54
Gwynne, Fred, 104, 105

Hackman, Gene, 81
Hall, Sam, 104
Hallat, Henry, 17
Hammer Films, 49, 51, 53, 54, 55, 56, 57, 59, 62, 83, 94, 101, 114
Hammer Horror Omnibus, 115
Harber, Harry Paul, 99
Hardwicke, Sir Cedric, 40
Hargitay, Mickey, 87, 89
Harrison, Harry, 114
Harwood, Ronald, 111
Hastings-Walton, Gladys, 17
Haunted Summer, 117
Hauser's Memory, 113
Hawthorne, Nathaniel, 73
Hawtrey, Charles, 83
Hayes, Melvyn, 53
Head, The, see *Nackte und der Satan, Die*
Heffron, Richard, 79
Heggie, O.P., 81
Heirs: The Workhouse of Filthy Creation, 107, 109, 111
Hell's Creatures, see *Marca del Hombre Lobo, La*
Henreid, Paul, 49
Herbert West—Re-animator, 113
Hija de Dracula, La, 86
Hinds, Anthony (John Elder), 54, 55, 56, 61

Hinwood, Peter, 94
Hitchcock, Alfred, 84
Hobson, Valerie, 32, 33
Hoch, Edward, 117
Holm, Ian, 104
Hombre que Vino Ummo, El, 85
Homunculus, 20, 21, 23
Horrible Dr Orloff, The, 86
Horror of Frankenstein, 57, 59, 61
House of Dracula, 45, 46
House of Frankenstein, 9, 43, 47, 54, 95
House of Freaks, 92
House on Bare Mountain, 70
Howard, Leslie, 27
How to Make a Monster, 65, 68, 69
HTV, 104
Hurlbut, William, 32
Hutchinson, Josephine, 38
Hutton, robert, 82

Ibbetson, Arthur, 106
I'm Sorry, the Bridge is Out, You'll have to Spend the Night, 18
Independent International Pictures, 79
Innocents, The, 55
I, Robot, 113
Isherwood, Christopher, 104, 105, 107
Island of Dr Moreau, The, 99, 113
Island of Lost Souls, 40, 113, 114
It, 84, 86, 87
I was a Teenage Frankenstein, 65, 66, 67
I was a Teenage Werewolf, 65, 66, 67

Jackson, Gordon, 111
James, Graham, 60
Janowitz, Hans, 21
Jesse James meets Frankenstein's Daughter, 73, 76, 77
Johns, Glynis, 70, 73
Jones, Carolyn, 103, 104
Jones, Freddie, 57, 90
Jordan, Glenn, 104
Journey's End, 27
Journey to the Unknown, 101

Karloff, Boris, 8, 9, 18, 21, 27, 28, 30, 31, 32, 33, 34, 38, 40, 42, 43, 44, 46, 49, 54, 65, 69, 70, 81, 90, 96, 103, 119
Kay, Roger, 70, 73
Kehoe, Vincent, 101
Keir, Udo, 92, 94
Kenton, Erle C., 40, 44, 47
Kid for Two Farthings, A, 101
King Kong versus Godzilla, 96
King's Road Theatre, London, 18
Kingston, Kiwi, 54, 55
Krauss, Werner, 21

Lady and the Monster, The, 115
Lady Frankenstein, see *Figlia di Frankenstein, La*
Laemmle Jr, Carl, 27
Lamont, Duncan, 54
Lanchester, Elsa, 32, 33
Landau, Richard, 104
Landon, Michael, 65, 67, 69
Landry, Gerard, 83
Lane, Ben, 103
Lang, Fritz, 21, 23
Laughton, Charles, 32, 113, 114
Leaky, Phil, 49, 51
Lederer, Francis, 99

Lee, Christopher, 49, 51, 52, 53
Lee, Rowland V., 37
Leslie, Fred, 15, 16, 17
Lewis, A., 104, 105
Life without Soul, 19, 24
Little Theatre, London, 17
Living Theatre, 18
Lizard's Leg and Owlet's Wing, 103
Lorre, Peter, 103
Lovecraft, H.P., 113
Lowe, Edward T., 43, 47
Lugosi, Bela, 9, 27, 28, 37, 38, 39, 42, 47, 49, 104
Lumière, Auguste *and* Louis, 19
Lust for a Vampire, 61

Mabuchi, Kaoru, 97
Mad Monster, The, 44, 45
Madrid, José Luis, 83
Magnificent Seven, The, 79
Mahon, Barry, 73
Malvern, Paul, 46
Man and the Monster, The, 15
Manners, David, 27
Man without a Body, 82, 83
Marca del Hombre Lobo, La (Frankenstein's Bloody Terror/ Hell's Creatures), 84, 85
Marlowe, Derek, 117
Marshal, William, 80
Martinez, Gilberto, 95
Marvel Comics, 119
Mason, James, 105, 106, 107
Matinee Theatre, 101
Maxwell, James, 54
Mayer, Carl, 21
McCallum, David, 105
McDowall, Roddy, 84, 86
McWhinnie, Donald, 111
Melford, George, 95
Mélies, George, 19
Metropolis, 23, 24, 25
Milner, H.M., 15
Mizer, Bob, 73
Moby Dick, 113
Model Man, The, 15
Monster and the Magician, The, 15
Monster World, 36, 112
Monstro di Frankenstein, Il, 19
Moore, Kieron, 84
Morrissey, Paul, 92, 94
Mosher, Bob, 104
Moxon's Master, 113
Muller, Robert, 104, 107
Mummy's Shroud, The, 56
Munster Go Home, 104, 105
Munsters, The, 103, 104
Murphy, Donald, 71
Myers, Robert J., 117
Mystery of the Marie Celeste, The, 49

Nackte und der Satan, Die (The Head), 83
Naish, J. Carrol, 79, 92
Naschy, Paul, 84, 85
NBC Television, 101, 104, 105
Neill, Roy William, 42
Nelson-Keys, Anthony, 56, 57
Night of Frankenstein, The, 114
Night Stalker, The, 104
Nilsson, Harry, 90

Norton, Edgar, 37
No Way to Treat a Lady, 104

O'Brien, Richard, 18
O'Brien, Willis, 96
Ocean Film Corporation, 19
O'Connor, Una, 32, 34
Ogle, Charles, 19, 20
O'Herlihy, Dan, 73
Old Dark House, The, 32
Onyx, Narda, 77
Orlak, el Infierno de Frankenstein, 95
Oscarsson, Per, 94
Owen, Beverly, 104

Pagett, Nicola, 106
Palance, Jack, 104
Parker, Edwin, 42
Parry, Michel, 117
Patrick, Butch, 104
Paviot, Paul, 49
Peake, Richard Brinsley, 15
Pearlman, Gilbert, 117
Phantom of the Opera, The, 27
Piccoli, Michel, 49
Pickett, Bob, 18
Pierce, Jack, 27, 28, 40, 46, 49, 54, 104
Pirie, David, 87
Poelzig, Hans, 21
Polanski, Roman, 92
Polidori, John, 11, 12, 117
Pommer, Erich, 21
Ponti, Carlo, 92
Presumption; or, The Fate of Frankenstein, 15
Price, Dennis, 59, 61
Price, Vincent, 73, 74, 75
Priest, Pat, 104
Prowse, Dave, 61, 63
Psycho, 84

Quatermass Experiment, The, 49
Quatermass II, 49

Rathbone, Basil, 37, 38, 42
Rennie, Michael, 85
Return of the Fly, 9
Revenge of Frankenstein, The, 54, 114, 115
Rice, Joan, 61
Richardson, John, 90
Richardson, Sir Ralph, 105
Rippert, Otto, 20
Rivals of Frankenstein, The, 117
Roald Dahl's Tales of the Unexpected, 108, 110, 111
Robinson, Bernard, 53, 56, 61
Robles, German, 95
Rocky Horror Show, The 18, 94
Rocky Horror Picture Show, The 18, 94
Rohrig, Walter, 21
Rosenberg, John, 111
Rosse, Herman, 28
Rothwell, Talbot, 83
Route 66, 101, 103
Royal Coburg Theatre, London, 15
Royal Court Theatre, London, 18

Salkow, Sidney, 73
Salmonova, Lyda, 23
Sangster, Jimmy, 53, 54, 57, 61, 114

Santo contra la Hija de Frankenstein, 96
Santos, Angel Fernandez, 92
Santo y Blue Demon contra los Monstruós, 95
Sarazzin, Michael, 105, 106
Sargent, Joseph, 79
Scars of Dracula, The, 57
Scott, Sir Walter, 14
Scream, Blacula Scream, 80
Screen Gems, 101, 103
Seal of Frankenstein, The, 114
Selig Polyscope Co., 19
Seymour, Jane, 105, 106
Sharman, Jim, 18, 94
Shelley, Mary, 9, 11, 12, 14, 18, 28, 30, 47, 49, 53, 62, 78, 92, 94, 95, 99, 104, 105, 111, 113, 115, 117, 119
Shelley, Percy Bysshe, 11, 12, 14
Simon, Michel, 83
Sims, Joan, 83
Single Summer with L.B., A, 117
Siodmak, Curt, 42, 113
Slaves of Frankenstein, The, 117
Smight, Jack, 104, 106
Smiley, Joseph W., 19, 24
Smith, Madeline, 63
Son of Dracula
  1943 version, 9
  1973 version, 90
Son of Frankenstein, 9, 32, 37, 81
Spirit of the Beehive, The, 90, 91
Standing, Percy Darell, 19
Starr, Ringo, 90
Steinruck, Albert, 21
Step of Frankenstein, The, 114
Stevens, Onslow, 45, 46, 47
Stoker, Bram, 9, 27, 94
Strange, Glenn, 44, 45, 46, 47, 48, 54
Strickfaden, Ken, 28
Stritch, Elaine, 108, 109, 111
Strock, Herbert L., 65

Tales of Frankenstein
  book, 117
  TV series, 101
Tales of Tomorrow, 101
Terror is a Man, 99
Terror of Frankenstein, 115
Testamento del Frankenstein, El, 83
Thames Television, 104
Theatre Upstair, London, 18
Thesiger, Ernest, 32
Three Musteteers, The, 37
Tibbles, George, 104
Toho Company, 96, 97
Torrent, Ana, 90, 92
Torticola contre Frankensberg, 49
Tower of Frankenstein, The, 114
Trip to the Moon, A, 19
Trivas, Victor, 83
Troughton, Patrick, 64
Tsuburaya, Eiji, 97
Twentieth Century-Fox, 101
Twice Told Tales, 73, 74, 75

Unholy Three, The, 27
Universal Pictures, 17, 18, 27, 28, 30, 32, 37, 38, 40, 42, 43, 46, 47, 49, 51, 54, 55, 80, 81, 90, 95, 104
Urquhart, Robert, 49, 52, 53

Vallis, George, 83
Vampiro y Compania, El, 95
Van Sloan, Edward, 28
Veidt, Conrad, 21, 22
Victor Frankenstein, 94
Villasante, José, 90, 91, 92
Vitali, Leon, 94
Vonnegut Jr, Kurt, 115
Von Stroheim, Erich, 115
Von Theumer, Ernst (Mel E. Welles), 86
Vorkov, Zandor, 79

Wallack, James, 15
Ward, Simon, 59
Warhol, Andy, 92, 94
Warm, Hermann, 21
Warner Brothers, 51
Warner, Jack L., 51
Warren, Barry, 56
Waterloo Bridge, 27
Webling, Peggy, 17
Wegener, Paul, 20, 21, 23, 24

Welles, Mel E., *see* Von Theumer, Ernst
Welles, Orson, 86
Wells, H.G., 9, 99, 113
Westmore, Bud, 104
Westworld, 79
Whale, James, 23, 27, 28, 30, 32, 33, 37, 49, 90, 117
Whiting, Leonard, 105, 106, 107
Wiene, Robert, 21, 70, 83
Wilder, Gene, 80, 81, 117
Wilder, W. Lee, 83, 101
William and Mary, 108, 109
Williams, Kenneth, 83
Wolff, Ed, 72
Wolf Man, The, 40, 42
Wollstonecraft, Mary, 11
Woodthorpe, Peter, 54
Woolf, Sir John, 111
Wuthering Heights, 113

Young Frankenstein, 80, 81, 117

Zucco, George, 44, 45